FORTY ACRES &
A RED BELLY FORD

THE SMITH FAMILY
of
CALLOWAY COUNTY

The **Clark** Group

Lexington, Kentucky

Clark Publishing, Inc.
dba The Clark Group
250 East Short Street
Lexington, KY 40507
800 944 3995 info@theclarkgroupinfo.com

Visit our Web site at www.TheClarkGroupInfo.com

First Edition: January 2011

Printed in the United States of America.
10 9 8 7 6 5 4 3 2 1

ISBN: 978-0-9832639-0-6

Book and cover design by Kelly Elliott
Back cover photo taken by Ulysses Hayes

To Henry and Lizzie Smith
For giving us this place we call home.

ACKNOWLEDGMENTS

*D*ad and I live a few hours apart, so we began this book with emails, phone calls, and the naïve expectation that we could actually recall enough family stories to fill a book! Yet those conversations continued ... and continued ... and eventually we began expanding our search, interviewing family members and searching out old records and photographs.

Though there were times we thought we might never finish, we wouldn't trade this experience for anything. How much fun to recall fond memories and figure out questions we'd always had about the Smith family and farm life in west Kentucky! And of course we couldn't have done it without our extended family. We would like to thank everyone who contributed stories and pictures. We also appreciate the many researchers who came before us, as their records enabled us to match up our family stories with actual events and occurrences.

Furthermore, we'd like to thank Diana Taylor of Taylor Gray Communications in Frankfort, Ky., who organized and edited the book, and writer Fran Ellers of Louisville, Ky., who proofread it for us.

Finally, a special thanks and recognition to the Kentucky Historical Society for the fellowship they provided. This small grant contributed to the research we were able to conduct, tying our family stories to Kentucky's history.

— *Bobbie Smith Bryant*

In *40 Acres and a Red Belly Ford: The Smith Family of Calloway County*, present-day Smith family raconteurs chronicle a realistic portrayal of ten continuous generations of Smith farmers. This saga describes a family that for 250 years has lived in the Jackson Purchase area of Western Kentucky. Their lives have been anchored to a cluster of farms within a 12 mile radius and continue today with 1,500 acres farmed by members of the family.

Information contained in survey histories we studied in high school and college is mostly limited to famous people, wars and major social movements. These histories fail to describe what it means when a farm family converts from horses and mules to a red belly Ford tractor, attends a revival meeting, makes a quilt, cooks red-eye gravy, smells a potbellied stove in a grocery store, watches a TV for the first time ever with a screen filled with snow, suckers tobacco on a hot August day, goes to a community hog killing on a cold Thanksgiving, and produces all they need to eat on their own farm.

The book provides us with a continuous recitation of oral family history and tales that seem oft-told, because they probably are. The modern day patriarch, Billy Smith, recalls one such incredible tale that occurred in the late seventies. A neighbor from an adjoining farm one evening suddenly came to his house, offering him a once in a lifetime opportunity to buy the adjoining farm. Seizing the opportunity, he wrote the farmer a check for $90,000, knowing that he had a meager $100 in his bank account. His encounter with the president of the bank early on the following morning is a hilarious story only rural and small town folk in that era could experience.

This story and many others like it point out the unique lessons of self-reliance and independence learned in the fields of rural America. Though the setting for the story is confined to a small county nestled in the rich alluvial soil of middle America, its lesson in learning responsibility, encouraging creativity and experiencing the overwhelming sense of belonging that exudes from this family is inspirational for those of us who have experienced it, and instructive for those who have not.

In this well written book the authors give credence to the Jeffersonian belief in the virtuousness of rural life and firmly dispel the idea that it is an archaic notion of a simpler time.

Instead of the "trapped" feeling often used by those who fail to grasp the genius of rural life, we find a family totally at home with modern day technology. They travel to all the world's continents, including Antarctica, and their offspring continue to use the skills they have learned on the farm to succeed in corporate America and the professions.

I highly recommend this book to anyone who is seeking to understand the creation of a family tradition that will engender in its members stability, a sense of belonging and a launching pad for a productive life.

— Sid Easley
Attorney and retired judge Murray, Kentucky

CONTENTS

Introduction   *1*

I   Coming to Kentucky   *11*

II   Family Culture and Traditions   *24*

III   War and West Kentucky   *43*

IV   Farm Modernization and Changes in Tobacco   *55*

V   Transportation   *85*

VI   The Importance of Education   *93*

VII   Harrowing Moments (on the Farm)   *106*

VIII   Lighter Moments   *118*

IX   From the 1950s to the 70s   *157*

X   From the 1970s to Today   *171*

Afterword   *183*

Bibliography   *194*

Index   *197*

INTRODUCTION

he Smiths have been farmers for more than 250 years, with 10 generations of the family living or buried within a 12-mile radius of the farm that continues operating today in west Kentucky. Today's Smith Farms include some 1,500 acres of soybeans, wheat, corn and dark-fired tobacco that are worked by two full-time, five part-time, and eight seasonal employees.

Smith Farms in 2007 with a growing crop of dark fired tobacco.

Farming has changed a great deal since our forefathers plowed their first furrow. Today, the farm they tilled with muscle and mule uses the most modern equipment and technology available to produce first-class crops. But certain fundamentals have remained unchanged through the centuries: the importance of family, the value of hard work, and the love of the land.

This book, combining the history of the family and the community it has called home for decades with the recollections of the current generation of Smiths, is meant to capture the story of the Smith family's legacy.

The Smith Family Lineage

Henry Smith was born circa 1760 of German descent. While his entry into America has not yet been clarified, he begins the tenth generation of our Smith lineage as we know it today. Henry and his wife, Elizabeth Staley (Stahli), and their families most likely traveled down the Great Wagon Road through the Shenandoah Valley of Virginia and Maryland, crossing the Blue

Henry and Elizabeth (Staley) Smith are buried in Soldier Creek Cemetery in Marshall County, northeast of Brewers.

Ridge Mountains somewhere near Roanoke and coming into the Piedmont region of North Carolina, settling in the area made up of Randolph, Rowan and Guilford counties. Henry and Elizabeth's children were Adam, Eli, Nellie, Barbara, Sally, and Hiram Absalom, our ancestor.

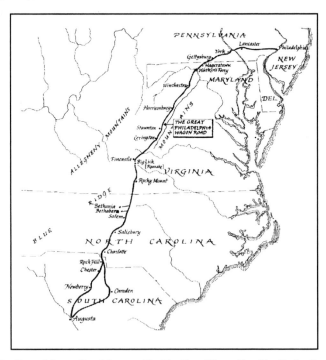

Map of the Great Wagon Road featured in *The Great Wagon Road* by Parke Rouse, Jr.

Hiram Absalom Smith, son of Henry and Elizabeth, was born circa 1800-05. He was married to Levina, and they had a family of four girls and four boys: Sara, Burton (our ancestor), Eliza, John, William, Elizabeth, Needham, and Mary Ann. The patriarch of the modern family, Billy Smith, remembers his grandfather, Raymon Smith, talking about *his* grandfather Burton Smith, relating the story of *his* father, Henry, and grandfather, Absalom, entering Kentucky with their families in the early 1800s, walking from North Carolina through the Cumberland Gap, looking for land to settle.

By 1830, the census reflected that the Smith family was living in the area of Calloway and Marshall counties. Hiram Absalom Smith, along with several other families, settled part of what is now Marshall County between Soldier Creek and Oak Level and between Middle Fork Creek and Graves County.

THE LAND GRANT

To all whom these presents shall come greeting, know ye that by virtue and in consideration of the sum of forty dollars paid into the Receivers office at Waidsboro agreeably to an act of Assembly approved the third day of January 1825 there is granted by this said Commonwealth unto Absalom Smith the North East quarter of Section seventeen Township Four, Range Three, each containing one hundred and sixty acres. With its appurtenances to have and to hold the said land a parcel of land with is appurtenances to the said Absalom Smith and his heirs forever in witness where of the said Thomas Metcalfe, Esquire, Governor of the Commonwealth of Kentucky hath herewith at his hand and caused the seat of the said Commonwealth to be affiance ... in the year of our Lord one thousand eight hundred and twenty nine and of the Commonwealth the thirty eight.

By the Governor, Thomas Metcalfe

Original land grant of Absolum Smith. *Kentucky Secretary of State website.*

A New County

Marshall County was formed from Calloway County in 1842. The General Assembly of the Commonwealth's assignments noted that Absalom Smith was one of the justices named in connection with this action; they met at the house of James Clark, about four miles east of the present site of Benton, on June 7, 1842, and formally organized the first county court.

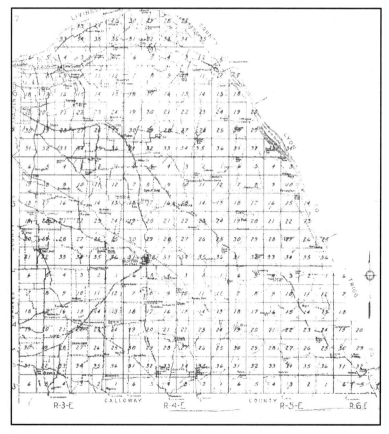

Original Marshall County land plat west of the Tennessee River, showing Absolum Smith's property at quarter section northeast, #17, range 3, township 4, east.
Map courtesy of the Marshall County Genealogy Society, History of Marshall County and the coordinates are from the Kentucky Secretary of State's website.

Burton Smith's will of 1890 features the division of his original land grant at the time of his death.

Burton Smith, son of Hiram Absalom Smith, was born October 29, 1830. He was married three times and had seven children, and census records indicate that he was a farmer. One of his sons, Needham Van Buren Smith, operated a horse-powered thrasher and was noted in local historical accounts as introducing a steam-powered thrasher to the community about 1885. In addition to Needham, Burton's children included:

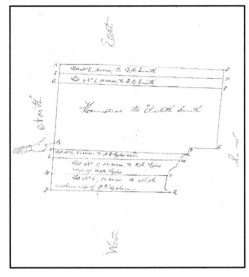

Rebecca L., Mary Elizabeth, William Aaron, Nancy Caroline, James Franklin (our ancestor), and Martha Adeline.

James Franklin Smith, son of Burton Smith, was born October 22, 1865. A farmer, he was married to Emma Grubbs, and they had five children: Rexie,

Photo features James Franklin Smith's family: Far left, grandson Hal Smith, James Franklin, wife Emma (Grubbs), children Raymon, Lillian, Rex and seated, Haleene and Delle.

Raymon (our ancestor), Lillian, Haleene and Delle. They were members of the Primitive Baptist Church at Soldier Creek. James Franklin died in 1930 and Emma in 1946.

Raymon Smith, son of James Franklin Smith, was born June 27, 1893. He was a farmer but also operated a grocery store in Mayfield for nine years before moving back to the Kirksey community. He was married to Gracie Wrather and they had two sons, William Hal (our ancestor) and James.

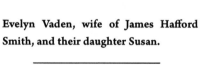

Raymon, Gracie (Wrather) and William Hal Smith.

Evelyn Vaden, wife of James Hafford Smith, and their daughter Susan.

James H. Smith was born January 10, 1920 and at the young age of 24, lost his life while serving in the Armed Forces in France. James married Evelyn before going to war and was never able to meet his daughter, Susan Smith Phillips. Susan now lives in Halls, Tennessee, and is married to Robert (Bob) Phillips. They have one daughter, Kelley Blair Phillips Kail, and two grandchildren, Joshua (Josh) Arnold and Johnathan (John) Robert.

William Hal Smith, son of Raymon Smith, was born June 26, 1914. Hal married Geneva Brewer and followed in his father's footsteps, farming and running a grocery store. The store was one of the first in the county to have

William Hal and James Hafford Smith

a television and the family made it available for all the neighbors to watch. They were of the Methodist faith and had two children, Billy and Bettie. Bettie married Gregg Stoll and they have two daughters, Sarah Stoll and Suzannah Stoll Szabo. Suzannah is married to Tim Szabo and they have a son, Zachary.

Bettie Smith Stoll, husband Gregg, daughters Suzannah and Sarah Stoll. Photo dated 2000.

Bettie Louise Smith, daughter of William Hal Smith was born September 1, 1942. Bettie's life has been filled with music as she taught music for 41 years in the public school system. Additionally, she has played the piano since childhood and continues playing for churches, weddings, funerals and all sorts of community and special events. She is married to Gregg Stoll and has two daughters, Suzannah and Sarah and one grandson, Zachary.

William Hal (Billy) Smith, Jr., son of William Hal Smith, was born April 2, 1937. Billy learned to farm from his father and grandfather and remains interested in the farm operations today. He was

William Hal Smith, Jr., wife Shirley (Chilcutt), son Billy Dale and daughter, Bobbie Ann. Photo dated 1959.

involved with Farm Bureau at the local, state and national levels, serving as a director and officer in all three as well as being employed in the fertilizer industry for 42 years. He was instrumental in integrating modern farm machinery and equipment as it came on the market after World War II while learning to use herbicides, pesticides, and fertilizer to full advantage. Billy has been married for more than 50 years to his high school sweetheart, Shirley Chilcutt Smith. They have two children, Billy Dale and Bobbie.

William Dale (Billy Dale) Smith, was born August 21, 1958, the son of Billy and Shirley Chilcutt Smith. He has been the Smith Farms owner and operator since 1982. Billy Dale knew at the age of 5 that he would be a farmer, following in the footsteps of his father, grandfather and great-grandfather, and started with his own tobacco crop around 1976 at age 18. Under his supervision, the farm has embraced

William (Billy) Dale, son Josh, and grandson, Logan Smith.

computerization and uses technology to a profitable advantage. Due to his commitment to current standards of operations, he is responsible for the farm continuing into the 21st century as a family farm operation. Billy Dale has two children, Josh and Janae.

Bobbie Smith Bryant, born October 28, 1959, sister of Billy Dale, provides marketing and promotional assistance as well as historic and genealogy research to Smith Farms. Bobbie is employed full-time with the Kentucky League of Cities and lives in central Kentucky with her husband, William Hamilton (Bill) Bryant, Jr.

William (Bill) Hamilton Bryant, Jr. and wife Bobbie (Smith) Bryant.

Joshua Job Smith, son of Billy Dale Smith and Sheila Kirk Smith, was born October 11, 1981. Josh works part-time with his dad on the farm; he purchased his first farm in 2009 and it adjoins Smith Farms. He is now producing eight acres of his own dark fired and air-cured tobacco. Josh is a teacher and football coach at Calloway County Middle School. He is married to Missy Jenkins Smith and they have two sons, Logan Brock and Carter Ryan.

Joshua Job Smith, wife Melissa (Missy Jenkins), Logan and Carter Smith.

Jacquelyn Janae Smith, daughter of Billy Dale Smith and Sheila Kirk Smith, was born May 4, 1995. Janae is a student in the Calloway County school system and an active Girl Scout; she also enjoys playing volleyball with her team. Janae's favorite part of the farm is riding the Gator.

Jacquelyn Janae Smith, photo dated 2009.

Logan Brock and Carter Ryan Smith start the tenth generation of the Smith family farmers. Logan and Carter are the sons of Josh and Missy Smith and were born September 3, 2007, and April 13, 2010, respectively. They are the delight of the Smith family, whose members hope they will love farming and carry on the family tradition in west Kentucky.

CHAPTER I

Coming to Kentucky

Kaintuckee—the name given to the area now known as Kentucky, meaning "dark and bloody land." Its origin is thought to be Cherokee or Shawnee.

❧❧

*I*n 1832, Henry and Elizabeth Smith of North Carolina gathered their family, loaded their possessions on a buckboard wagon and headed west. They were on their way, along with thousands of other pioneers, migrating through the Cumberland Gap into Kaintuckee. They had purchased land in the Jackson Purchase area in 1825 and made the decision to move and settle there with their families.

The Smiths were of German heritage, most likely descendants of Protestant refugees who fled the persecution of Louis XIV of France and escaped from communities near the Rhine River region of Germany to seek religious freedom in America. Upon arriving in the New World, the family is believed to have traveled the Great Wagon Road through the Shenandoah

Example of pioneer wagon. *Courtesy Wikipedia*

Valley of Virginia and into the Piedmont region of North Carolina. They were part of the mass migration of German-speaking people who moved into the area between 1745 and 1750.

The number of farmers increased over time, prompting the need for more land. The migration continued into areas opened up by Daniel Boone and other pioneers who came through the Cumberland Gap to settle the abundant lands of Kentucky and Tennessee. They found fertile soil with tall trees, lush grass, and plentiful sources of water. They eventually moved quite a distance from the Cumberland Gap—away from the mountains to flatter land further west.

Example of log homestead in Kentucky.
Courtesy Kentucky Historical Society

———————

Settlers would cluster together to help one another with building homes, raising barns, harvesting crops, and sewing. Farmers from birth, they adapted quickly to the new ground and soon had tobacco and grain crops in production. They also understood the value of cow manure as fertilizer and used it to their advantage.

The settlers and their families had few possessions and only the bare necessities for comfort. As Parke Rouse, Jr. notes in his work *The Great Wagon Road*, the settlers made their own furniture, farm equipment, and clothing, and often cooked in iron pots that sat on three-legged stands or hung by chains from a beam or iron bar built into a chimney.

From these humble beginnings, the Smiths built a life as farmers. Henry and his sons began buying property, settling close to one another in what would become Marshall and Calloway counties in west Kentucky. They established their homes close to Soldier Creek, a tributary of the west fork of Clark's River.

Public land survey grid of Marshall County. *Courtesy Marshall County Genealogy Society, The History of Marshall County.*

The rectangular system of surveying is used for all United States public lands surveys. The first step is establishing an initial point in the area. Through this point, a north-south line (Principal Meridian) and an east-west line (Base Line) are run. Guide lines are run every six miles east and west from the Principal Meridian marking strips called Ranges. A similar set of lines is run every six miles north and south from the Base Line cutting the Ranges into squares, six miles on each side, called Townships. These are numbered from the Principal Meridian and the Base Line: Township 1 North, Range 2 West, etc. Townships are subdivided into thirty-six squares, one mile on each side, called Sections, which are numbered from the northeast corner of the Township moving west and then east alternately. Sections, containing approximately 640 acres, are the smallest tracts that the law requires to be surveyed.

Marshall County has an area of 324.5 square miles.

Elevations: Gilbertsville about 339 feet; Aurora 350 feet; Brewers about 480 feet; Briensburg 457 feet; Scale 432 feet; Palma 430 feet; Sharpe 417 feet; Benton about 450 feet.

EARLY TRANSPORTATION

Little noted but important to the early settlers were the river ferries that provided an alternative form of transportation to the buckboard or farm wagon. By 1819, several ferries were established on the Tennessee River in west Kentucky. According to the Kentucky Encyclopedia, most ferries of that day were pulled across the river after the boat was attached with a sliding hitch to a rope or metal cable extending from bank to bank. This was known as a current ferry because the rope or cable was used to counter the effect of the river's current.

| 13 |

Over the years, the Smith clan settled within 15 miles of one another, helping each other build homes, sheds, smoke houses, corncribs, outhouses, and milk barns. Today's Smith Farms are still within those early property boundaries.

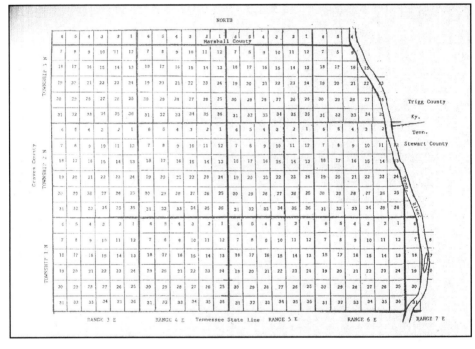

Calloway County land survey showing Burton Smith's property located in the northwest quarter section #30, range 5, township 2, east. Henry Smith's property was located at the northwest quarter section, #16, range 5, township 1, east. *Courtesy Kentucky Secretary of State website.*

The *Story of Calloway County*, written in 1980 by Dorothy and Kirby Jennings, noted that Calloway County had one of the largest percentages of home ownership in the nation as well as one of the highest percentages of college degrees per capita. Farming was the main source of income for virtually all the early settlers, who sought good soil for their crops.

Many of the pioneer farmers brought along their own cattle, chicken, cows, and goats, providing meat and other necessities. Small game was in abundance, including deer, rabbit, possum, quail, doves, raccoon, and passenger pigeons.

Poultry was a major activity in the county as many farm wives kept chickens as a source of both food and revenue. Country stores and city establishments would accept eggs and chickens in payment for merchandise and services—even newspaper subscriptions. Local historians note that the egg was a significant rival to the silver dollar in the early days.

COMING HOME TO ROOST

Chickens have been part of the Smith family history. Billy Smith remembers his grandmother, Lois Robinson Brewer:

"Mama Brewer had a round cane egg basket. She would also make butter with an old-fashioned churn. She would put her eggs and homemade butter in the mule-drawn wagon and go to the store to shop for necessities.

Lois (Robinson) Brewer, wife of Sam, feeding chickens at their home place in Kirksey.

If she picked up more than her eggs and butter were worth, she would put back the least liked or needed item because she said she had no money to buy it outright."

The Smiths bought land in and around what is known today as the Kirksey community in Calloway County. Kirksey, located 10 miles northwest of Murray, was established by that name in 1871 when the first post office opened. Legend has it that residents of the community had met and chosen two possible names for the town—Reidville, in recognition of a prominent local family with the name of Reid, and Rosedale, due to the abundance of roses along the fences leading into town. As fate would have it, however, local store operator Stephen Kirksey submitted the application for the post office and listed his own name. Early businesses in the tiny village included a casket

Kirksey General Store, *photo courtesy Johnny Gingles.*

factory, tobacco processing facilities, a general store, several feed mills, restaurants, two saloons, a wood carving factory, a popcorn sheller and buyer for a packaging company and the Kirksey Bank.

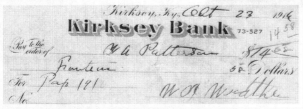

Bank note from Bank of Kirksey, signed by William Wrather, father of Gracie Wrather Smith.

Tobacco was an important cash crop for the settlers, as it was for many generations that followed. It is likely that tobacco seeds were among the farm products that our ancestor, Henry Smith, brought to Kentucky from North Carolina. As different tobacco varieties were grown, one type emerged from the unique combination of Kentucky soil, climate and water: dark fired tobacco. This heavy-type plant, broad-leafed and intensively cultivated, was much stronger with nicotine than any other variety grown in early America.

The farmers learned very early that the thicker the leaves were, the more nicotine the finished product would have. They achieved the goal of thicker and heavier leaves by topping the plants (breaking out the blooms).

Dark fired tobacco barn from turn of the century, located in Penny. *Photo dated 2010.*

The Smiths, like most farmers of that era, provided for their families by growing row crops and tobacco. Men, women and children literally worked from sunup to sundown tending the crops, always hoping for a good growing season. They counted on tobacco yielding the cash that the family needed to put food on the table and shoes on the children. Early settlers in the county grew tobacco for export, shipping the crop by steamboat down the Tennessee and Mississippi rivers to New Orleans, where it would head to the international market.

The tedious work of growing tobacco began with preparation of the plant beds. In early February the beds would be burned, then sown with seeds saved from choice plants of the previous year. The beds were covered with canvas to protect them and to control plant growth until setting time. When conditions were right, plants were pulled by hand from the beds and placed in tubs in preparation for setting.

Dark leaf tobacco being shown at Smith Farms by Bernadino Ruiz, an H2A worker from Guanajuato, Mexico.

Sample tobacco bed, *courtesy of the Kentucky Historical Society.*

In the spring, men would begin clearing the land, guiding a plow behind a sturdy mule or horse. Each row was then defined by hoe. Workers brought plants from the beds and, using a hand-hewn wooden peg, stooping or bending over to place the plant or crawling along the rows putting each plant in place about 40 inches apart. This backbreaking work was just the beginning of the long and arduous growing process that was repeated year after year. (More details about the production of tobacco and its importance to the family can be found in later chapters.)

As the men worked in the fields, the women in the family would take care of the daily chores around the house. That pattern continued through the generations, and much of the work involved the preparation of food—most of it home-grown—for the hard-working field hands. Billy Dale recalled:

Ladies taking food to the field, left to right, Sheila (Kirk) Smith, Bobbie (Smith) Bryant and Shirley (Chilcutt) Smith. *Photo made in late 1970s.*

"My great-grandmother, Mama Brewer, would ring the old iron dinner bell when it was time for dinner to get Papa in from the field. I remember one day at dinner time, Momma, Granny, and Mama Brewer had prepared the most elaborate meal, with two flatbed wagons full of food. We probably had 15 to 20 workers. It was the last time that I saw food in the field like that, sometime in the late 1960s. This is the same day that Daddy got too hot and had to go to the hospital (one of several harrowing events that are detailed in a later chapter)."

Farm life could be monotonous, even uneventful from year to year, with entertainment provided by the occasional political campaign and election or church revivals that were held when an itinerant preacher arrived in the community. Seasonal work offered opportunities for social gatherings in the form of everything from barn-raising to quilting bees as families gathered with their neighbors for support, entertainment and, at times, their very survival.

Granny Smith (Geneva Brewer Smith) spoke often of her paternal grandmother, Dovie Sutherland Brewer, who married James Irvin Brewer when she was only 12 years old. Granny said: *"Grandma Dovie supposedly had her first son, Uncle Carl, only four days after she turned fourteen. She then had a baby every two years and wound up with six boys and one girl."*

Grandma Dovie would weave wool into cloth and make all her children's clothes. As each of the boys married, they would bring their wives to live with them until they could get enough money together to buy their own place, each then living within a few miles of the family home. Dovie taught

Jim and Dovie (Sutherland) Brewer with their sons, Carl, Clay, Irvin, Samuel, Jodie, and Clyde. (Children not shown in photo include son Pat who died in 1895 and daughter Linnie who was not born until 1904.)

each of the wives how to weave and make wool, and they created a blanket or quilt before leaving to live on their own.

The earliest settlers had little fabric to work with but were in need of warm bedcovers, so they saved every scrap of fabric and usable portion of worn garments that they could. Even very small remnants could be used for patchwork quilts.

In some ways, a patchwork quilt became a record of a family's history, incorporating bits of garments and such other household textiles as flour

Nine patch quilt made by Lois (Robinson) Brewer, sometime in the 1920s or '30s.

and feed sacks. Although quilt making was primarily a useful art, the practitioners turned the necessity into social occasions with quilting parties and quilting bees. These gatherings let the women work together to finish a quilt while the men and children visited, ate, and played games.

Quilting has long been part of the Smith family history, the skill passing from one generation to the next. Shirley Chilcutt Smith told how her mother, Rubye Maynard Chilcutt, first taught her how to quilt:

"She had learned very early before she and Dad were first married. Back then they had what they called 'Quilting Bees' in their neighborhood. Most all families in their neighborhood would set up quilting frames made of wood, then screw hooks into the ceiling in a six foot square to hang the wooden frame on with ropes. This was done so they could let the entire frame down to work on a quilt and then pull it back up, close to the ceiling when they finished for the day, so it wouldn't be in the way of daily living when they were not using it to quilt in their home.

The Homemaker's Clubs with all their families would visit each neigh-

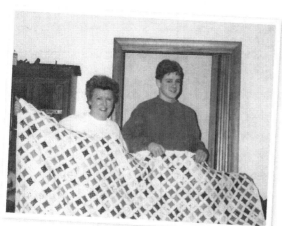

Shirley (Chilcutt) Smith showing her first quilt in the cathedral pattern, made for grandson Josh Smith in 1994.

bor's house within a reasonable area in a pre-arrangement, so that all the families interested and those who lived close by could finish their quilts in the winter time when they couldn't do anything else. This was a good way to help each other meet a need and keep up with all the neighborhood happenings at the same time. They also enjoyed each other's company and passed the time off in a valuable way for each of them as well.

My family really excelled with this talent as we still have some very beautiful and durable quilts to admire and enjoy because of what they did back then. When I got married, my mother-in-law, Geneva Smith, was an excellent seamstress and worked at the garment plant in Murray for many years. She helped me learn to truly enjoy sewing and I still do today, some 53 years later."

Food Traditions
The less you have to eat, the more you know about cooking.

❦

Members of the Smith family, much like their neighbors, were experts in making the most out of the harvest each year. From corn, wheat, oats, and soybeans to garden vegetables, fruits, and nuts, the family cooks knew how to prepare and preserve food so the family would have enough to last through the harsh winter months. Billy Dale has vivid memories of how his great-grandmother canned and dried apples:

"Being at Mama Brewer's when she was cutting up apples was a real

Lois (Robinson) Brewer holding granddaughter Bettie Louise Smith at their home on Rob Mason Road in 1946.

experience. She'd string bed sheets out in the trees, on all the outbuildings and sheds, everywhere there was a flat spot. She would spread the sliced apples out in the sun to dry. It would take a while, but she made sure we always had something good to eat, no matter what time of year it was."

In addition to apples, other fruits such as cherries, peaches, pears, plums, and strawberries were canned, preserved, or dried for winter use. Food preservation was accomplished differently in that era before refrigeration, when salt was used as a preservative. Many techniques were learned from the native Indians, especially how to dry corn. *The Kentucky Encyclopedia* notes that corn was a pioneer staple—milled, roasted, boiled, or baked. It was a basic ingredient in bread, porridges, cakes—even whiskey.

Canning began as an effort to feed the army during the Civil War, according to *Kentucky Hospitality: A 200 Year Tradition*. After the war the Cooperative Extension Service of the federal Department of Agriculture helped to accelerate and improve home canning.

Memories of early Kentucky food preparation would be incomplete without country ham—preserved through dry salting or sugar curing. Kentucky's hams are renowned throughout the country. The basic curing process used in Kentucky originated in England and, in the old days, salt would be boiled down from brines at

Bernice Wisehart showing off country hams cured by Gibson Locker Plant for generations in Calloway County. Photo taken from Hutson Chemical Company brochure in the 1980s.

one of Kentucky's plentiful salt springs. Because Kentucky's hams differ considerably from one region to another, recipes vary as well. Today's Smith family members still enjoy a hearty breakfast with delicious country hams or sausage, fresh eggs, homemade biscuits, and sawmill or red-eye gravy.

CARE AND COOKING OF WEST KENTUCKY COUNTRY HAM

The uncooked cured country ham should be placed in a cloth bag intact, in a heavy grocery sack, tied very tightly at the top and hung in a cool, dry place. If it should develop mold, scrub it off when you are ready to use the ham.

To serve, slice the ham into steaks, 3/8 inch thick or less. Soak the steaks in milk, water, juice or coca cola for at least 30 minutes. Trim the rind and any excess fat. Put the ham in a heavy frying pan and cover with water. Simmer slowly until the water is gone. Lightly brown the ham on both sides and remove from the pan.

SMITH FAMILY RED-EYE GRAVY

Save the drippings of grease from cooking a ham or browning ham slices when fried. Use 1 tbsp. corn starch per cup of water and/or drippings and lightly sprinkle salt and pepper into the drippings or cooking oil, stirring constantly to prevent from sticking. This is best done in an iron skillet. The corn starch thickens it rapidly so stir well. Pour into a gravy boat or over biscuits and serve immediately, while hot.

CHAPTER II

Family Culture & Traditions

*I*n *Agrarian Kentucky,* Dr. Thomas Clark notes that the first cabins were hardly raised before log schoolhouses, churches, lodge rooms and society halls appeared in rural parts of the state. Early churches were largely congregational in nature, and activities followed the seasonal farming calendar. Clark points out that the church in Kentucky has rarely represented more than 35 percent of the state's population, but attendance might have indicated otherwise as the church provided opportunities for entertainment and socializing that attracted local residents hungry for a break in the daily pattern of work.

In *The Story of Calloway County,* Kirby and Dorothy Jennings note that several congregations were formed in Calloway County, the first being organized at the original county seat of Wadesboro. Among the first denominations: Methodist, First Christian, Presbyterian, and Mormon. A log house was the county's first place of worship and a circuit rider supplied the sermons. Smith family members were, for the most part, either Methodists or Presbyterians.

Reva and Geneva Brewer (Smith) are the two girls in the middle of the top row at the Little Rock School which was located between Stella and Kirksey. *Photo taken sometime in the early 1930s.*

In 1852, a Methodist church named Little Rock was organized in the Kirksey area. Although the location of the first meeting place is unknown, records show that Z.P. Reed deeded land one mile south of Kirksey to the Little Rock Church. A log house on the site was used as a church until a two-story frame building was erected there in the 1860s. In 1901, the congregation moved the church to the site of the current Kirksey United Methodist Church, in the heart of the community. The name was changed when the church separated from Little Rock School.

The 1901 church building was destroyed in 1928 (cause undetermined) to be replaced by a new frame structure housing a sanctuary and five Sunday school rooms. An annex was added in 1958 to accommodate a growing congregation and additional renovations were made before 1959, when a brick church with expanded Sunday school rooms, kitchen and restrooms was opened to the congregation and community.

Kirksey United Methodist Church congregation.
Photo taken in 1936 and provided by Joe Pat James.

This little church at Kirksey has been part of the Smith clan for many generations. The earliest record we have is from the early 1950s, when Raymon and Gracie Smith returned from living in Mayfield and joined the

Kirksey United Methodist Church. Six generations later, their great, great, great, grandsons Logan and Carter Smith attend the same church with their mom and dad, Josh and Missy Smith.

Billy Smith recalled:

"The Methodist Church was always a big part of our lives. There was one preacher that stands out as my favorite, and his name was John Jones. He came to Kirksey when he was married and had two kids. He was not a country boy but he was a Christian man and loved his work as a preacher. He motivated several of us and we all worked in the church,

John, Nadine, Greg and Diane Jones. John was pastor at Kirksey United Methodist Church in the 1960s.

built up the membership, and decided to build a new parsonage for our preacher. That took place in 1971, and we also built an addition on to the church in 1983. Both of our children were members there."

Kirksey United Methodist Church parsonage committee. Left to right: Shorty Johnson, Billy Smith, Baron Palmer, Hershel Pace, pastor John Jones, and Lubie Parrish.

Bobbie Smith Bryant recalled church activities and relationships while growing up:

"Several of our school classmates attended the same church, so we not only went to grade school together, but we had Sunday school

Kirksey United Methodist Church 1973.

together as well. As we got older we had an active youth program and the adults always paid close attention to us and our activities. They kept us involved and engaged with learning about the scripture, and applying it in real-life ways.

Max and Mavis Hurt at their 50th wedding anniversary celebration at the Kirksey United Methodist Church.

There were many nice people that we loved at the church, but there was one couple in particular that were very special to our family and the Kirksey community as well as the entire county. Max and Mavis Hurt were well-known elders who had been part of the congregation very early on. Mr. Hurt was the principal when Hal and Granny were at Kirksey High School. He had also worked nationally with the Woodmen of the World and had lived in Omaha, Nebraska, for many years, retiring back to his home place at Kirksey.

My favorite memories of him are the hand written notes, cards and letters he sent to me from the time I was just a young child of 4 or 5 up until he died, when I was in my 20s. I still have every one of them as they were treasured keepsakes for me. He would send me those notes each *time I did even the smallest thing in church, from memorizing a scripture verse, visiting a nursing home, or standing in to speak as a lay pastor. I would have done anything in this world to impress or please that man as he was so positive and encouraging to me.*

Miss Mavis, as we all called her, was always in the church choir, along with my Granny and several others. She was so nice, too, very supportive of everything that happened in the church. We loved both of the Hurts dearly. I guess their memory has stuck with me through the years because even today, my husband, Bill, and I have a grey striped cat who, for whatever reason, reminded me of Miss Mavis, so that is what we named her!

Bettie Smith Stoll.

Another thing I remember at Kirksey Church was when our Aunt Bettie Smith Stoll (Daddy's sister) would come home from Paducah and go to church with us. The church organist would always relinquish the organ or piano for Aunt Bettie to play. She is so talented; I still love to hear her play, particularly the church hymns from years ago.

Our family has lots of great memories from our little church. Momma was the nursery teacher for years, particularly when Josh was born, up until she and Dad moved to Kansas City. I also remember that Sunday mornings were Daddy's day for making breakfast for us. He'd make pancakes with sausage or bacon ... a special treat, just on the weekends. He and Momma were also very clear about the responsibility of tithing. I remember to this day that they would write out the church check and leave it on the desk each week so it would be ready to take on Sunday morning.

One other Sunday morning ritual that stands out in my mind was the times when we'd spend Saturday night with our grandparents,

Hal and Geneva (Brewer) Smith at their store in Kirksey in the early 1950s.

Granny and Hal Smith. When Billy Dale and I were little children, Hal had his grocery store in Kirksey. It was naturally the gathering place for all the older men in the neighborhood to come around the old stove, smoking their cigars or cigarettes, drinking coffee, and telling tales. Granny would get us up at 4:30 or so on Sunday morning so we could go with Hal to open the store. Hal would keep the store open from 5 a.m. until 8 a.m. on Sundays. This would give her quiet time to get Sunday dinner cooked for the whole family to come to their house after church.

After Hal sold the store and he and Granny had moved to their house north of Kirksey, Hal would drive us to the store and give each of us a quarter so we could buy whatever candy or cold drinks we wanted. I still remember the smell of that old pot-bellied stove and the cigar smoke hanging in the air. The old men would tease me, but just enough so I knew I was safe and happy in being around them."

Granny's Never Fail Sunday Dinner Rolls

1 pkg. dry yeast (put into 1/2 cup warm water)	1/2 cup sugar
1/2 cup shortening, melted	2 cups milk
1/4 tsp. salt	3 cups flour

Mix dry yeast, sugar, shortening, milk and salt. Add enough flour to make a stiff batter. Let rise in bowl until double in size. Punch down and knead, adding flour until elastic. Roll out, cut and place in a buttered pan. Butter well on top. When they are double in height, they are ready to bake at 425 degrees for about 20 minutes.

Raymon Smith's home and grocery in Mayfield, Graves County in the mid 1940s.

The country store, such as the ones that Raymon Smith ran in Mayfield and his son Hal ran in Kirksey, were, and remain today, a focal point for neighbors to keep up with local news and gossip. "The stores and their keeper were institutions within themselves," Dr. Clark tells us in *Kentucky: Land of Contrast*. "The storekeeper was better informed than anyone else in a community. There was a constant babble of gossip among his customers. They sought credit and revealed their economic plights. In trouble they sought the storekeepers' advice and the malcontents fussed at him because of high prices for what they bought and the low prices they received for the products they sold to the store. Nevertheless, the stores were places which exercised strong institutional influence over their communities."

Billy Smith told more about Papa and Mama Smith and of how the country store evolved in the Smith family:

"*In the early 1930s, Papa and Mama Smith were living northeast of Kirksey on their farm. Mama Smith had an eye disease called glaucoma and lost one of her eyes and had damage to the other one. As Mama Smith was blind, I remember as a kid and a young adult she would always ask us to come to her and let her feel of our head and shoulders and arms to see how big we had become and she always wanted to feel of Billy Dale, Bobbie and then Josh. She then would brag to everyone on how healthy and pretty we were.*

As her blindness got worse, she and Papa decided to rent their farm to Ocus Lawrence, a cousin to Mama Smith, and they moved to Mayfield. Papa Smith bought a grocery store

Hal's store in Mayfield, Graves County.

Raymon and Gracie (Wrather) Smith's home in Kirksey.
Photo taken in mid 1940s.

on 9th Street in Mayfield with living quarters upstairs. This was a lot better for them than living out in the country on bad roads with no electric power or other city conveniences. This was also much easier on them as the doctor and hospital were close by. Mother and Dad also lived in Mayfield at that time and they could help see after her. By the mid 1940s Papa Smith sold his store and moved back to the farm at Kirksey.

My dad had also gone into the grocery store business sometime in the early to mid 1940s in Mayfield. He enjoyed it but after his parents had moved back to Kirksey he wanted to be closer to them as his mother was in bad health. He sold his store in Mayfield in 1951 and rented a store building in Kirksey.

In the spring of 1951 we moved to Kirksey and moved into the building Dad had rented. It had ten rooms up stairs, five on each side of a hall that ran from the front to the back of building. The downstairs had two rooms—the front room was about three times the size of the back room. The front became the store and the back became the storage area. There was a small room on the backside of building that was a barber shop where John Cunningham cut hair on Saturdays. This was where I got my first flat top haircut and my first burr.

After I became an adult, I was really surprised how well Mama Smith could cook and clean house as she was legally blind. She always made a green relish that I thought was the best ever, and after Shirley and I married we would always have Christmas dinner at Papa and Mama Smith's. As far as I know today she did the entire dinner on her own as Papa Smith was as lost in the kitchen as I am. The Smith men only seem *to know where the kitchen table and chairs are, so Shirley says, and I think she is probably right."*

Susan Smith, daughter of James Hafford and Evelyn (Vaden) Smith.

Susan Smith Phillips enjoyed the good home cooking too:

"She always canned pickles in the summer and kept them under the house where it was cool or in the pantry under the stairs. She made the best homemade pickles I ever ate and to this day I can still taste those wonderful sweet pickles. She also made a delicious apple pie that I have never tasted duplicated. I don't know how she did it or what the ingredients were.

I have wonderful childhood memories of Papa and Mama Smith and the store at Kirksey. I can remember riding to Uncle Hal's store in Kirksey with Papa Smith in the wagon with the horses. I must have been awfully young. When I got older he had a '49 Ford I think and I was always begging him to let me drive it which he never did. When I would go to their house, sometimes in the fall and sometimes in the summer, she would always have Dr. Peppers in the big tall bottle for me up in the tray under the little freezer so they would be good and cold.

Susan had other vivid memories as well:

"Did you ever see her take her glass eye out? It was always amazing to me that someone could do that. I can remember us swinging on the back porch and me begging her to take out her glass eye and she always would. Isn't it strange the things you remember when you are young."

Billy went on:

"*After Papa Smith died, Dad moved Mama Smith into a trailer in his and mother's back yard. She lived there until she had to go to a retirement center. Mama Smith spent the last 20-plus years of her life in an assisted living center. She loved country ham all her life and when her great, great, grandson Josh was a youngster, he and I would take her a country ham and biscuit on Saturday mornings. She would smile as she proceeded to try and chew the country ham, all the while saying what a wonderful young man Josh was for coming to visit with her.*"

᠀᠀

Bettie Smith Stoll remembered growing up living over her parents' grocery store in Kirksey:

"*Whenever my mother needed anything from the grocery, I would just run downstairs and get it for her and run right back upstairs with it. Whenever my parents got out of the grocery business in Kirksey, it took a while to think about making a grocery list before going to the big grocery stores in Murray.*"

Inside Hal's store at Kirksey.

᠀᠀

Billy Dale Smith also had fond memories of Hal's store at Kirksey:

"*What I enjoyed most about Hal's store was I'd get to drink a Chocolate Soldier or a grape NeHi, or a Coke, and I didn't have to pay for them. There were always racks of candy and we could get what we*

wanted. I remember that John Cunningham had the barber shop right
next door, and I'd get my hair cut every Saturday for one dollar. I think it
was that price for as long as I could remember.

When I was really young, Granny and Hal lived upstairs over the
store for a while and I remember the long hall with the rooms on either
side. There was a small car mechanic shop on the back side of the grocery
on the north end. When they sold it, I bought a bunch of my tools from
him and I've still got them today."

Billy Smith recalled:

"After we moved to Kirksey in 1951, the television was just beginning
to be viewed in this part of the country. If you had a tall tower with the
right kind of antenna, you could pick up a station in St. Louis, Memphis
or Nashville. About all you could do was see a blurred, snowy picture and
hear the sound. Mother and Dad operated the general store and when
television first came out, they bought one and put it on the counter in back
of store, close to the old Warm Morning coal stove. On Saturday nights,
people would come to the store, sit around the stove, and try to watch the
Grand Old Opry from Nashville or a base ball game from St. Louis. The
picture was in black and white and the reception from Memphis was just
about impossible. These were the good old days."

Billy Dale Smith had one painful memory:

"After Hal sold the store he still had his meat slicer at the house. For
some reason I thought I should see how sharp it was. I laid my finger on it
and of course split it wide open. Needless to say, I haven't done that again."

~ ~

Some farms in rural Kentucky produced crops other than corn,
soybeans, wheat, and tobacco, offering varieties of fruits and vegetables. Billy
Dale Smith remembered a buying trip to one orchard:

"When I was 4 to 6 years old, Bobbie and our friends Martha and
Margaret McCallon went with their mother, Datha, and our mom to

Mathis' Orchard in Mayfield to buy peaches. While we were there, there was a great big older man with all white clothes on, just like Colonel Sanders.

He picked at me and picked at me and tried to buy me for a quarter. He kept offering Mother money and he kept on teasing with me until I was afraid Mother was going to sell me and send me home with him.

A few years, later Dad got a call at work from a man who wanted to rent a 300-acre farm to him that used to be a cattle farm. He'd retired and the fellow that had rented it from him was leaving, so he wanted Dad to rent it. The

Joe Dunn and his family.

man that owned the farm was Joe Dunn and come to find out, that was the man that'd tried to buy me when we went to that peach orchard!"

🌾🌾

Kentucky: Land of Contrast reveals "…in early Kentucky there were great masses of rural folks who never heard any form of music except that made on fiddles, jew's-harps, strap organs and an occasional piano. Many churches were without a musical instrument, sometimes because members of congregations looked on them as evil and distractive things."

In the early days of Calloway County there were social gatherings called moonlight parties. *The Story of Calloway County* tells us, "Moonlight Parties were a pastime handed down from one generation to another in Calloway for it was a common source of entertainment among farm families the latter part of the 19th century. It was strictly a social event for neighborhoods covering as much as two square miles. Music was provided by fiddle players and guitar pickers. The young folk would gather in long lines with hands clasped about the waists of one another, keeping in step with the music.

Moonlight parties diminished in popularity as ice cream socials and pie or box suppers came on the scene, usually sponsored as fundraisers by local churches or schools. Local musicians and their harmonies were popular at these events.

Granny Smith told of her father, Sam Brewer, and several of his brothers who played in a string band:

"When Papa and his brothers lived at home there was a blind man that came to live with Grandma and Grandpa. He was a music teacher and he came there to teach them how to play instruments. He stayed the winter and taught the boys in exchange for room and board. Uncle Carl and Uncle Clyde played violins, Uncle Irvin and Uncle Joe played guitar, Uncle Clay played banjo and Papa (Sam) played mandolin." (As told to Shirley Smith by Geneva Brewer Smith in 1994)

Left to right: Sam Brewer, his father Jim and brother, Clay.

Billy Dale Smith treasures the hand-made mandolin that belonged to Papa:

"In the winter time he'd get it down from a shelf on the wall and play for me."

☙❧

Pearl inlay mandolin passed down to Billy Dale Smith, great-grandson of Sam Brewer.

Entertainment was also provided by the occasional circus. According to the *Story of Calloway County,* a circus—or Wild West show with Indians and animals—would come to town about once a year. Local business people frowned on the big show, seeing it as competition for limited local entertainment dollars. But it was popular, starting with the free parade that began at the big top, travel up Main Street to the Court Square, make the round and return to the tent.

Billy Smith loved the circus:

"I would slip off from school and go watch them unload the elephants and other animals. I always said when I was a kid that I would join the circus when I got upset with Mother and Dad. I never did, but I continue to take our kids and the grandkids to the circus almost every time it comes to town. I look forward to taking Logan and Carter if Josh will let me and if I am able. Loving the circus as much as I did—I always wanted a monkey. I still love to watch monkeys at the circus or at the zoo. I still think I would enjoy having a monkey as a pet."

❧❧

Funerals are part of the social fabric of any community. The *Story of Calloway County* tells us that in the part of the burial process involved a member of the bereaved family taking a measurement of the deceased by using a switch to draw the exact line for the length of the casket. The switch would be carried by a family member, standing upright in an open two-horse wagon to the cabinet maker. The appearance of a man with the switch on the wagon meant that a death had occurred, and onlookers knew immediately to share in the mourning. No words were needed.

Neighbors would help to excavate the plot for burial, sit up through the night with the body, usually within the home of the deceased, attend the funeral services and then help cover the casket with dirt. The first horse-drawn hearse wasn't used until 1896; before then, a mule drawn-wagon was used to take the coffin from the home to the burial plot.

Some people might ask why folks would sit up all night with the deceased. The reason was simple—and practical. Before embalming became the norm, family members and neighbors had to stay close to the body to keep cats, dogs, mice and rats away from the casket.

Granny Smith shared the following memories in 1994 with Shirley Smith:

"I can remember going to my Grandmother Bertha Neal (Wilson) Robinson's funeral when I was about 5 years old, in December of 1920. This was the very first funeral I ever remember going to. I sat on my Uncle Talmadge Robinson's lap in the front seat. It was a spring-type seat up on top of the horse-

Bertha Neal (Wilson) Robinson with husband James Polk and children, Talmadge, Lois and Bruce.

Hearse at the Churchill Funeral Home in Murray. One of three that they used from the 1860s to the mid 1900s. *Photo courtesy Kenny Imes at Imes-Miller Funeral Home in 2010.*

drawn hearse. That hearse is still on display next to J. H. Churchill's Funeral Home in Murray.

My sister, Reva, was 4, and she sat in Papa's lap (Sam Brewer), beside Mamma (Lois). Our Grandpa, James Polk Robinson, was in the rear seat of the hearse. The corpse was carried inside the carriage below the seats."

Aunt Bettie's CD of favorite hymns, dated 2002.

Funerals as well as regular church services offered an opportunity to share in singing hymns from old-time religion. The *Methodist Song Book* and other sources remained popular with the Kirksey congregation over many generations. Standard songs include *The Old Rugged Cross, When the Roll is Called Up Yonder, At the Cross, Bringing in the Sheaves, Onward Christian Soldiers, Amazing Grace, Rock of Ages,* and *Just as I am.* Aunt Bettie Smith Stoll created a piano collection of these favorite hymns in 2002 on compact disc as a gift to each of the Smith family.

Smith family members, top row left to right: Robert, Paul, Gracie (Wrather), Sue (Paul's wife), Rex, Delle and James Smith. Middle row, Haleene Smith, Emma (Grubbs) Smith, Emma's two sisters, Lovie and Ida, and Bessie (Rex's wife). Bottom row, Raymon Smith, William Grubbs (Emma's brother) and Hal Smith.

The Smith family has its own vernacular expressions, typical of the early settlers who were of Scot-Irish, English, and German ancestry. *The Kentucky Encyclopedia* notes that the mixture of different dialects contributed to the development of new and distinctive pronunciations as well as to the number and variety of words found in the state's folk vocabulary. The regions of the state reflect the diversity of the English language spoken here.

We're not sure about other places, but there are a few words and phrases that seem to have stayed with our family through the years.

Addled: Used to describe one who is out of sorts or not right in their head, as in "He came back from the war a bit addled."

Catty-cornered: A term often used to describe an object or a piece of furniture placed in the corner of a room.

Dirt Dauber: Another name for a wasp.

Dreckly: We'll take action soon, as in, "We'll get to these stories dreckly."

Eatchet: A question as to whether you have eaten recently.

Feedin' the Hands: The noon meal is usually called 'dinner' on the Smith farm, and feedin' the hands refers to serving the noon meal out in the field.

For Pete's Sake: We never knew for sure who Pete was, but this expression was to show frustration when something wasn't going just right.

Galavantin': A word that refers to moving about, going from place to place, as in "He was out galavantin around instead of coming home."

Got a Hitch in Yer Git-a-long: When an individual has a pain and can't move around easily.

Handy Work: Term that refers to skilled sewing, knitting, crochet or quilting. "She did lovely handy work."

High Horse: Meaning that someone was being a show off or misbehaving. "He'd best get down off that high horse if he knows what's good for him."

Hemmed and Hawed: To pause during conversation, searching for the words one would like to say.

Hissy Fit: A reflection of one's mood when one is angry. In other words, "She threw a hissy fit over tearing her dress."

I'll Swan: An expression or response when one is not sure what else to say. One of Granny Smith's most frequent comments.

In a huff: Also refers to ones' mood when agitated. "He left in a huff when he found out he couldn't get what he wanted."

Fair to Middlin': an expression that indicates that not all is well, as in: How are things with you? Oh, just fair to middlin'.

Flew the coop: well they just up and left, flew the coop! Chickens sometimes leave their coop for unknown reasons and never come back.

Gulley Washer: Good Lord at all this rain, it's a real gully washer, hope it doesn't drown our 'terbacker.

Jack–leg: What a tradesman is called when his skills are not quite up to par. "He's a jack-leg plumber."

Lickin' Yer Calf Over: Do it right the first time, or you'll be licking your calf over again.

Lord Have Mercy: Exclamation when uncertain what else to say to a situation.

Month of Sundays: Tells of the passage of time. "We hadn't seen grandpa in a month of Sundays.

Nigh-on: Refers to someone approaching something, as in: "He was nigh on to 100 before he passed."

Passel: This word was used when referring to some large amount. "He had a passel-full of corn in that load."

Pole Cat: Another name for a skunk.

Poke Sallet: Poke is a wild weed and some farmers would cook it much like spinach.

Reckon: A response such as when one supposes: "I reckon I'm alright."

Scarce as Hen's Teeth: Something quite rare.

Shet: To get rid of something, "To get shet of."

Sight More: A few more. "He had a sight more leaves in his box than I'd thought it would hold."

Skeeter: Mosquito.

Spittin' Image: When one individual looks much like another. "That little girl is the spittin' image of her daddy."

Stiff as a Poker: Dead. "Look at that bird, it's as stiff as a poker."

Terbacker or 'Backer: Country word for tobacco.

There's Frost on the Pumpkin: Description for light frost on the ground, or to reflect that a person is growing older.

Tizzy: To describe excitement such as, "They came a running to the house, all in a tizzy!"

Uppity: Snobbish.

Whompy-jawed: When something is not squared.

Worde Out, pronounced with long o sound: Tired. As a young boy Josh Smith learned this saying from his Papaw Chilcutt, "I'm just worde out."

Yonder: Expression for distance or place, as in "Over yonder."

CHAPTER III

War & West Kentucky

Civil War

*A*lthough there are no records of our ancestors' active involvement for either side during the Civil War, they apparently did have connections to the military in the form of the Kentucky State Guard. According to historical accounts, the original settlers of west Kentucky brought with them from Virginia a militia system, originally designed to defend against Indian attacks. The militia was no longer considered useful after the Indian wars were over, and it was effectively abolished in 1854.

"The Enrolled Militia of Marshall County Kentucky 1860-1876," compiled by the Marshall County Genealogical and Historical Society, notes that the Kentucky State Guard was organized as a volunteer militia beginning in 1860-61. It was widely perceived as working toward Kentucky's secession from the Union, and Unionists formed rival Home Guard companies. Both groups sought to attract recruits and obtain weapons but stopped short of fighting each other.

From 1860-76 the Kentucky State Militia lists show that several of our early ancestors, including Henry, Absalom, John, Needham and Burton, signed up for service.

However, there are no records indicating that our ancestors were actively involved in the Civil War, a time of great disruption for the family and the region. Kentucky was a state divided as the war broke out and remained that way through the conflict. An 1885 account by J. H. Battle, H. H. Perrin and

G. C. Kniffin, *Kentucky: A History of the State Embracing*, reveals the sentiments of some west Kentucky residents:

"Many of the people of the Jackson Purchase feel that they are placed at a serious disadvantage in respect to their proper rights and privileges under the state government. With this feeling strongly implanted in their hearts, they have hoped for years that they might join with the remainder of the Purchase in Tennessee, and thus form a State whose government would be more immediately identified with their interests. So strong had this feeling become during the late Civil War, that in May 1861 a convention was held in Mayfield, at which the proposition to secede from Kentucky, was earnestly discussed and recommended. The great support given the Confederate cause during the Civil War is a strong proof of the growth of this sentiment."

Confederate monument at the Court Square in Murray. *Photo source: Wikipedia*

This passage is of particular interest because, more than 150 years later, many residents of west Kentucky still believe that state government, located a few hundred miles away in central Kentucky, is not sensitive to their needs. To this day when Billy Smith gets upset with the powers that be in Frankfort, he shares his opinion that west Kentucky, the boot hill of Missouri, the northwest counties of Tennessee and the southern tier counties of Illinois, should secede from their respective states to form the 51st state, as none of them seem to get any attention from their state capitals.

Calloway Countians were for the most part sympathetic with the South during the war. The county, not strategically located, was not the site any active military operation. There were only a few slight skirmishes, and those were between small parties of opposing forces that periodically passed through parts of the county.

Calloway Countians were found carrying both the stars and bars and the stars and stripes. County records vary, but it appears that about 500 of the approximately 1,800 men who would have been eligible for the military joined the army of the Confederate States and about 200 joined the Federal army. Although there was little damage in the county, except that caused by guerilla raiders, many gave their lives for both causes. There were few slaveholders in the county.

The bitterness of Civil War lingered in the community long after the war ended. Historians reveal that the social wounds did not really heal until the opening of the Murray State Normal School some 60 years later. The divisiveness that affected people during the war hung on through the years and reared its ugly head in a frightful way, just after the turn of the next century in an event known as the Black Patch War.

The Black Patch War

Growing tobacco was back-breaking work. But farmers needed the income that the crop provided to feed, house, and clothe their families. As the 20th century dawned, more and more farmers in the dark-tobacco producing counties of west Kentucky and northwestern Tennessee became suspicious that they were being cheated when they took their crops to market. The reason: declining prices offered by the American Tobacco Company, a monopoly owned by James B. Duke.

The American Tobacco Company was charged by the federal government with conspiring in a free market to hold down prices. The frustration prompted farmers to organize into the Tobacco Planters Protective Association. The result was economic warfare against the eastern tobacco buyers. The struggle became bitter, even causing fights between neighbors, father and son, brother against brother. The three-year conflict, beginning in 1905, was known as the Black Patch War; its "soldiers" were called Night Riders. The Planters Protective Association counted as members about 20,000 farmers who grew dark fired tobacco; association officials disavowed any connection with the Night Riders, also sometimes called the Silent Brigade.

Night Rider mask on display at the Pennyroyal Area Museum located in downtown Hopkinsville.

Wearing masks and conducting their raids after sundown, the Night Riders terrorized both buyers and growers—using intimidation, threats, terrorism, and sometimes murder to force farmers into the Association and to coerce tobacco buyers to purchase only from the cooperative. The Kirksey community was clearly a hotbed of activity for these acts of violence.

On February 22, 1908, the *Murray Ledger and Times* reported on the first act of violence attributed to the Night Riders in Calloway County. The following narrative is taken directly from the article:

"*Brandon Hurt, who lived about a mile and a quarter from Kirksey, was visited by night riders on a Saturday night. His only tobacco barn was destroyed by fire. All telephone lines were cut about a mile out of Kirksey to prevent any communications in the neighborhood where Mr. Hurt lived. It was not known how many composed the party. Mr. Hurt was a well-known citizen of the county and had raised a crop of tobacco the last year. He had sold*

Night Rider newspaper article from Daily New Era in Hopkinsville, on display at the Pennyroyal Area Museum.

1908 New York Times full page article about the Night Riders in Kentucky.

and delivered the crop a few days before the fire occurred. He was not a member of the Association."

As news of the barn burning spread, fear and uncertainty gripped the people of Calloway County. The incident marked the beginning of a reign of violence that lasted through the Night Rider years, according to *The Story of Calloway County.* Calloway Countians became fearful and suspicious, even of their next-door neighbors, since no one knew the identities of the men behind the masks. The fear was evident in a letter that County Judge A.J.G. Wells wired to Governor A.E. Wilson in 1908:

"...The raids are almost nightly occurrences. No citizen is safe. Through all of these weeks, I with my fellow officers vigilant. While we have information that might become important in the future, we have not as yet been able to procure sufficient evidence upon which to make an arrest. I have definite and direct information from the riders themselves that before the moon changes they shall swoop down on Murray and burn her property and beat her citizens and continue to beat and drive the farmers over the county and burn their property forsooth they did not obey the mandates."

Murray Ledger and Times April 2, 1908

Instead of fighting back, the Calloway County farmers began to insert letters to the Association in the local paper, making it known that they would no longer sell their tobacco individually. By doing this, they hoped to ensure the safety of themselves and their families. One such letter was written by Dave Morgan:

"I desire to say that I am a friend of the Association and have always been. It is true that I have sold my crop of tobacco because I had to meet my obligations by the first of November. On the night of February 17, the night riders come to see me, but I did not think much about it. On the night of the 28th, they came again, about 50 or 60 in number, and let me know that if I did not comply with their orders what they would do to me. Now I want to say emphatically that I will put my tobacco that I raise in the Association. I hope that I have said enough for the satisfaction of all concerned, Dave Morgan."

Murray Ledger and Times March 8, 1908

Lawlessness prevailed in the area until Governor Wilson declared martial law and used the state militia to fight the marauders and take control of the area. Mounted soldiers patrolled county roads each night, the clip clop of horses' hooves starting at dusk and fading away at dawn. Not since the Civil War had residents been as anxious or frightened.

A HISTORIAN'S DESCRIPTION

In writing about the Night Riders and this dark time in Kentucky's history, Dr. Thomas Clark reveals in Agrarian Kentucky that "Royal monopolies, American trusts, soulless corporations and inept and cowardly Kentucky politicians all stood in farmers' eyes as threats to a once proud social and economic tradition. Night Riders bared in fictional form the fears, suspicions and hatreds of men bound in poverty to the single cash crop—tobacco. They could see little beyond the white-sheeted plant beds of uncooperative neighbors, of the next growing season and of their own curing barns. In furious night charges "possum hunters' left behind scraped plant beds as evidence of their enraged determination, which was still more tangibly impressive in the red glare of burning barns and tobacco warehouses.

"In Frankfort fear mingled with expediency. The burley belt smoldered at heart with the fires of revolt. The courts were castrated by intimidation of the night-riding warriors. In Frankfort sat a spineless governor who had reached office by an act of violence, but was incapable of positive action even had times been normal. Segments of the Kentucky press lacked courage to speak out against the excesses of vigilantism because they feared retaliation."

The turmoil that was created by the armed forces began to calm down as farmers started preparing their land for a new season's crop. But even with troops in the area, arson was still prevalent and was blamed for the destruction of a block of stores in Murray as well as numerous properties within the county. The militia was posted in

State Militia guarding Milton Oliver's tobacco patch in Christian County in 1911. Mr. Oliver was a witness in the Night Rider trial in Christian County. *Photo courtesy William T. Turner, Christian County Historian.*

the community from April until early December, disrupting the social, economic, and spiritual lives of the residents. The troops were finally ordered to break camp in 1908 with an agreement between growers and buyers, whose monopoly was partially broken. Disgruntled Night Riders continued their violence into the next year, finding themselves confronting armed citizens who were angered by their tactics. Soon afterward, dissension among members of the Growers Association helped end the fighting for good.

The conflict reflected elements of the Civil War—pitting brother against brother in violence. It also is interesting to note that the members of the Association were considered sympathetic with the Confederacy and were identified with the Democratic Party. Non-members were more closely identified with the Union and the Republican Party.

While those involved remained silent, Billy Smith remembered both of his grandfathers talking a little about the Black Patch War and the Night Riders:

"I was told by both of them, at different times of course, about the other one being for the Association or the other one not for the Association. By all means this topic was never discussed around the dinner table or at any family

Expecting the Night Riders. *Photo courtesy of Johnny Gingles.*

get-together. It was simply not talked about in our generation. After my parents passed away, we found an old picture of three young men sitting on the front stoop of the Kirksey Store with rifles or shotguns by their sides, looking as though they were waiting for somebody or something. Though it has never been publicly proven or admitted, my Uncle Gratis Wrather was suspected to have been one of the members of the Night Riders. Uncle Gratis was my

Gratis Wrather, brother of Gracie (Wrather) Smith, World War I.

grandmother Smith's brother. All I know is that Uncle Gratis went to Detroit very early in his life, joined the army in World War I and then worked for Ford Motor Company until he retired and moved back to Calloway County."

Billy Smith also recalled his parents telling him about what the families did about selling or not selling their tobacco.

"With this information, I think I knew which side they were on. I was surprised that the Smith side was against the Association and that the Brewer side was on the side of the Association, or the Night Riders. I would have thought it would have been the other way around, just knowing how each one of them believed and lived their lives. They would have been in their early teens and probably did not get involved in any of the trouble-making. I do not have any history of any involvement that their parents might have been doing during this time."

Every part of the community was touched by the conflict—even people who never grew a stalk of tobacco felt the terror of the times. The Story of Calloway County notes: "In the final analysis of retrospect, it is easy to see why both sides thought as they did. The Association was bound by a death oath to uphold the convictions of the group. They were looking at what would be best for all by letting the supply/demand concept dictate the price of tobacco.

As a result of the Association's efforts, prices paid for tobacco improved dramatically, rising 50 to 100 percent within two years. However, tobacco-buying companies were put out of business, leaving many farmers with stored tobacco that they could not sell. The depression that followed in Calloway County rendered the Association useless because it lacked a sound financial footing.

World War II

As World War II broke out, Calloway County experienced the hard times as much as larger communities. Billy Smith recalled:

"My early childhood memories in the very early 1940s consist mainly of World War II stories and nightmares. I can remember that Mother

and Dad would hang blankets and other items over the windows when the government would have blackout nights. This was supposed to keep the enemy from seeing what and where the citizens were located. I also remember that lots of items were scarce and the government issued books of stamps. You had to have so many stamps to purchase certain items. Some of the things that required stamps were sugar, coffee, tea, gas, rubber items like tires, and other things like shoes. I know that Mother and Dad had a hard time keeping up with them.

They had a battery radio and no electricity, and we could listen to the Grand Old Opry for one hour on Saturday night. I also remember sitting around the radio listening to news stories about the war, going to the movie house, and seeing newsreels about Germany and the South Pacific. For a 4- to 7-year-old boy this was quite scary."

Gracie (Wrather) Smith with son James Hafford Smith.

Many native sons went off to fight, including a member of the Smith family. James Smith, son of Raymon and Gracie Wrather Smith, was a private in the 95th Division. He was killed on December 1, 1944, in the Battle of the Bulge. In the service for two years, James left behind his parents and brother, Hal, and a wife, Evelyn Vaden, and baby daughter, Susan Smith Phillips, who now lives in Halls, Tennessee.

Billy Smith recalled:

"I vividly remember the night my Uncle James went off to war as it was the last time any member of the family was to see him. Our family gathered at the train station in Mayfield as the train came from Paducah and stopped there. I remember Papa and Mama Smith, my

James Smith.

Letter sent in 1944 from James Smith to his brother and sister-in-law shortly before his death during WWII.

daddy and Aunt Evelyn were all crying as they said goodbye. It was a very big deal for a 5-year-old boy. Uncle James was killed in action in France and was buried there. After the war was over they brought his body back home. By then Papa and Mama Smith had sold their store in Mayfield, moved back to Kirksey, and built a new house.

I remember the funeral well. At the funeral home, they let my dad look in the casket and then they transferred the casket to my grandparents' house, just north of Kirksey where they lived. I remember that my Grandmother Smith was stone blind at that time and how hard it was for her to accept the death of her second son. The funeral was the following day at the Kirksey Methodist Church, and he was buried at the Brewer's Cemetery in Marshall County, just three miles from where the first

Uncle James' casket at the Raymon Smith family home in Kirksey.

three generations of Smiths are buried. That's just about five miles from where we are today at Smith Farms."

By all accounts, 1946 brought an end to horse and buggy days on the farm. An industrial surge in the Calloway County economy was prompted by new types of machinery. Many farmers started taking jobs with the new industries, reducing their farm work to part-time.

CHAPTER IV

Farm Modernization & Changes in Tobacco

*P*rogress was in the air as time began to heal the wounds from the Black Patch War. Census records dating to the early 1800s indicate that all the Smith men were, for the most part, farmers. We learned that Needham Van Buren Smith (grandson of Henry, son of Burton Smith) operated a horse-powered thrasher and introduced a steam-powered thrasher to the community about 1885.

Wheat powered thrasher, *photo courtesy the Kentucky Historical Society.*

The wheels of time left visible tracks in the cultural and agricultural growth of the Kirksey community. Steam power and the wheat thrasher it fueled gave way to modern combines. With these technological advances came other developments, including new roads and progressive mechanical operations.

World War I involved a number of young men from Calloway County and brought with it the changes of a new era. World War II, and the Great Depression between the two wars, also shaped the farming practices and technology.

❧❧

Road bed from Murray to Benton, *photo courtesy the Kentucky Historical Society.*

County citizens rallied around and put gravel on the road from the Marshall County line to the city of Murray by way of Wadesboro. Not knowing whose idea it was, in 1913 the editor of the *Murray Ledger and Times* wrote about an idea where every interested man in the county contributed two days of work, two days of mule-team labor or $6 in cash to the project. The names of all willing participants—along with the size of their donations—would be published in the newspaper. October 15 and 16 were the designated work days, with 400 animal teams and up to a thousand men armed with picks, shovels, wagons and pond slips gathered for what became known as the 3M organization: Men, Mules, Money. The newspaper account asserted that the event outshone any three-ring circus ever held in the region. Working from dawn until well past sundown, the workers completed half the job in the two days.

The newspaper editor called for a "whole-hog repeat performance" on the Wadesboro road to complete the job, asking for a duplication of each man's work, mules or money from the first effort and ordering all "wallflower and bank sitters to steer clear as there was no place for the loud mouths who don't know how to work!"

Citizens involved in the first "road show" were troubled by the notion that other parts of the county could steal their glory, so the repeat performance mirrored the success of the first. Within three weeks, thousands of citizens cheerfully participated in the successful project that set a precedent for similar efforts: a Murray-to-Paris road, built with the help of Southside

Road crew working in Calloway County.

residents and the promise of donors' names being printed in the newspaper; a Kirksey-to-Murray road built by Kirksey residents; and other road projects in nearby counties.

The Great Depression

The dark days of the Great Depression brought hard times.

According to *Kentucky: Portrait in Paradox*, the tobacco market, inflated by the war, went into a sudden decline. A drought struck in 1930 and extended into the following year. Calloway County went for a month and a half with no rain at all that fall. Crops wilted, animals died, people suffered and farms withered away. Times were incredibly tough on farmers in this time of trial.

Billy Smith remembers Papa Brewer telling him how on New Year's morning in either 1931 or 1932 that he and his family were told to leave the farm they lived on as the bank had sold it:

"He said he hitched the mules to the wagon, put Mama Brewer and the two children, Geneva and Reva, in the wagon, tied the cows to the back of the wagon, put the chickens in a coop on the wagon, and started going west towards Mayfield. They got as far as Grandpa Brewer's house just east of Mayfield and he let them live in an outbuilding across the road until they could get on their feet and buy a place of their own. This is the place that I caught the goat when I was a very young boy. They moved west of Mayfield in the early 1940s."

Challenges continued throughout the decade, as Billy Smith recalls:

"Dad had graduated from Draughn's Business College in Paducah, and he and mother married in 1935. Being right after the Great Depression there was not much hope on the farm, and Dad got a job driving a milk delivery route in Mayfield. Mother worked in the Five and Dime Store and

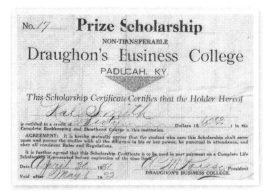

No. 17   **Prize Scholarship**
NON-TRANSFERABLE
Draughon's Business College
PADUCAH, KY.

This Scholarship Certificate Certifies that the Holder Hereof

Draughn's Business College scholarship for Hal Smith.

I remember she would almost always bring me a small toy home from work on Saturday night when she was paid. Some time around my age of 4 to 6 years old, Dad got into the grocery business, he and Mother operated the little store there in Mayfield.

There are several memories of that time. My grandparents lived about three miles out in the country, and I liked to spend the weekends with them. One Saturday Papa came to the store in a wagon pulled by two mules. The wagon had a springboard seat in it and they let me go home with him in the mule-drawn wagon.

They had chickens and I loved to help them feed the chickens. There was one downside: her old rooster would always run me back into the house. One week when I was staying with them, my cousin, Jo Nell, was visiting at the same time and we were out in the yard playing. That old rooster chased us both into the outhouse. We were both so scared and we had to stay until Mama Brewer came hunting for us."

Billy Smith and cousin, Jo Nell Story, daughter of Harvey and Reva Brewer Story.

OUTHOUSES

Outhouses were in almost universal use in the early decades of the 1900s, both in town and in the country. *The Story of Calloway County* reports: "In 1910 the city of Murray passed a bond issue to finance a water works system. Despite its passage, there was extensive opposition challenging the wisdom of permitting inside toilets in the city. The very idea of constructing privies within households was an unnerving proposition for a society accustomed to the great outdoors for such needs for thousands of years. Disdainfully, rural people frowned upon such a concept of progress, further widening the gap between farmers and townspeople with such outlandish ideas."

Typical outhouse. *Photo source: public-domain-photos.com*

Bobbie Smith Bryant recalls that, even when she was a young girl in the early 1960s, some rural homes, including that of her great-grandparents Lois and Sam Brewer, still did not have indoor plumbing.

"Papa and Mamma Brewer would let us spend the night in their upstairs bedroom and they didn't have a bathroom up there. She didn't want us trying to go up and down the stairs during the night so we had a chamber potty that we were to use. She was so good to us; she never once had me to clean it up after we'd stayed overnight."

It was during these difficult times that a new tobacco pool was formed by President Roosevelt and Congress. The Dark Fired Tobacco Association, headquartered in Murray, allowed a more relaxed marketing process for

Tobacco Sales Row showing buyers as they walk and buy. *Photo courtesy William T. Turner, Christian County Historian.*

farmers. Auctions were held on the two loose-leaf warehouse floors, where U.S. graders would assign grades indicating the quality of the crop. Farmers would allow their tobacco to go to the highest bidder or to the new co-op by accepting the association's advance grade price.

THE FARMERS PROBLEM
KIRKSEY HIGH SCHOOL ECHO
JUNE 30, 1929

The KHS Echo, June 30, 1929.

The greatest problem with which the farmer of today is confronted is the problem of converting the investment or debt into credit. A greater percentage of the farming class of people pass away from this world showing a small amount of material accomplishments than any other class of people. This is mainly done because they make their debt consumptive instead of productive. Other industrial men have been awake for many years and have sought a means whereby the production of their business far exceeds the cost. This has been made possible by replacing old, inefficient, unproductive facilities such as machinery, buildings, transportation facilities and the like by the

1922 Kirksey High School.

more modern implements, in other words, they have broken away from the century ago beliefs and have adopted the scientific developments. The same change MUST be brought about among the farmers and it is now in its youth but growing very slowly.

How does the work of scientists help the farmer? Space does not permit detailed explanation of the above question, but by scientific investigation and analysis, the farmer's problems are solved. He only has to discard all his superstitious theories and apply facts. All such information, as the plant food requirements in the different sections of the country, the kind of fertilizers best to use, proper cultivation, breeding animals to be more efficient as well as scientific feeding of animals. All market conditions such as the amount of any commodity produced as compared with the amount of the same commodity consumed, the transportation cost, etc. All this information is available at the State Agriculture Experiment station, or the U. S. Department of Agriculture.

The time is coming soon when the less efficient farmer will be automatically replaced by those who are more capable and willing to adjust themselves to the necessary conditions, in order that farming may be run on a more profitable basis. The opportunity is before you, take advantage of it.

The New Deal Administration and, to a lesser extent, the Farm Security Administration, revealed how archaic and inefficient many of Kentucky's farming practices were 175 years after settlement. Three new federal policies encouraged a change in land use policies and practices. The Civilian Conservation Crops focused on reforestation, terracing and erosion control, and building farm access roads. The Soil Conservation Administration and the Tennessee Valley Authority conservation program began a major revolution in the protection of Kentucky's lands, according to *A History of Kentucky.*

Kentucky: Portrait in Paradox 1900-1950 describes such New Deal programs as the Agricultural Adjustment Act (AAA), which provided funds to refinance farm mortgages. The AAA asked farmers to reduce production in return for subsidies, thereby establishing and maintaining a basic price. That meant a 28 percent reduction in the size of the 1935 tobacco crop. The AAA was reorganized in 1938 with tobacco and corn quotes and price stabilization programs that farmers found more acceptable.

SOME THINGS TO THINK ABOUT—CALLOWAY NEEDS COUNTY AGENT

A SHORT EXCERPT FROM AN ARTICLE IN THE JANUARY 1930 ISSUE OF THE KIRKSEY HIGH SCHOOL ECHO

During the past few years farming methods in Calloway have improved. We are recognized as a progressive agricultural county. You know the story of our fame as a dairy county. Farmers are trying to improve their farms through the use of lime and legumes. Quality has been stressed to tobacco growers. Just when everything was working around for

1930 Kirksey Echo

a better day for the farmers, we lost our county agent. Farmers are in an inquisitive attitude; they want to know about happenings in regard to their business. While farmers are in this attitude of mind it seems to me that any delay in getting an edge will be expensive.

It is coming to be considered as essential to have a county agent as any other county official. For the sake of our school, our organizations and our progressive programs, let's get together, employ a good county agent, get behind him and his program and keep things going forward.

Party Lines

Over the years, technological advances brought improved telephone systems to the Kirksey community. While rural phones had been available since early in the 20th century, only 8 percent of Calloway County's population had telephones by 1908, the sets hanging on a wall with dry cell battery power and a single line transmission. Fragile poles connected one household to the next, and the party line phone provided great entertainment for farm folks. Receivers or earpieces would click along the line indicating that someone else was listening in. The practice was not considered ill-mannered—just a way of life.

Billy Smith remembered:

"When I was a young kid, we lived in Mayfield and had a party line telephone. Each one on the party line had a certain ring (some two short rings or two long or one ring, etc.). Once the telephone quit ringing, the neighbors would pick up and listen in on the conversation. Out in the county the farmers' wives would listen in on the calls, and sometimes they would

Crank style telephone, *courtesy William Hamilton Bryant, Jr. family.*

all get on the line and visit for a while with each other. This was their way of keeping up with what was going on in the neighborhood.

The telephone system had operators located in an office with a switch board. When you picked up the phone to call someone the operators would ask you for the telephone number that you wanted to call and they would hook you up to the number that you gave them. This number would ring on all the phones that were on the party line.

Sometime in the mid to late 1950s we went to dialing our own telephone calls with the old spin type dialer. That was about the time the telephone number had the prefix added or the first three numbers (PL3-6166). Then we went to area codes and direct dialing nationwide and eventually to world-wide calling. Now we have the Internet, so no telling what will be next."

In the early 1950s the Rural Electric Corporation agreed to finance construction of a rural telephone cooperative to serve the areas of the county not served by Southern Bell Company. By the late 1950s Southern Bell installed a modern flash system of direct communication with a central office in downtown Murray. Most former telephone operators were left without jobs as a result of the technological upgrade, but subscribers seemed very happy with the new system.

Billy Dale Smith recalled Mamma Brewer's crank-style phones and her use of the party line:

"When she lived at Penny, I remember her listening in on other people's conversations. She'd put her finger up to her mouth to shush me. I remember picking up and listing in, too, both at her house and at Granny's."

In 1968 Southern Bell divided its huge organization with county subscribers being assigned to a new county co-op exchange. Amazing as it seems, West Kentucky Rural Telephone Cooperative was still providing one-party service in the Kirksey area in 1975, when a $3 million federal loan put an official end to the party line.

Cars and Tractors

As the country slowly recovered from the Depression, word came that the Ford Motor Company was paying workers $5 a day, a wage much higher than the average and an amount that Calloway County men could scarcely imagine. A migration of county folk to the North ensued, enabling many farmers to pay off debts back home with their Ford paychecks.

Gratis Wrather with fancy new car.

Billy Smith recalled:

"Mamma Smith's brother, Uncle Gratis, worked at Ford in Detroit, up to the time he retired and then he moved back to Calloway County. When I was a teenager and in high school in the early 1950s there were a lot of local families who had kinfolk working in Detroit for Ford. In fact, some of my high school friends went to Detroit and started bringing used cars back to Calloway County to refurbish and clean them up for resale. Several of them got their financial start that way. Ford was a financial savior for a lot of families in West Kentucky. In the 1950s until the 1970s Calloway County reportedly used as much DuPont paint as Detroit did and was considered the used car capital of the U.S.A."

Motorized vehicles showed up in Kirksey in 1910 when the *Murray Ledger and Times* reported

Smith's with car, left is Hal, James, Gracie and Raymon.

that C. O. Gingles had purchased a 20 horsepower Ford machine that proved to be a disturbing mode of transportation to the mules and horses of Kirksey. Soon, an onslaught of Model Ts invaded the community and the technology found its way into farm machinery as tractors began to take the place of mule- or horse-drawn machinery.

Billy Smith remembered very well two stories about early-model tractors:

"Papa Brewer had bought an old steel-tire case tractor and disc. He was disking a field down in a creek bottom. The old tractor started to get hot and he had to pour water in it to keep it cool. After two or three stops to walk to the creek with a bucket to get water, he decided that this would be a good job for me. He gave the bucket to me and told me that while he drove the tractor another round that I could go to creek and bring water back to him. This was the job for me the rest of afternoon. On one of his stops, he killed the engine and as we were pouring the water into the radiator, we heard a noise up in the sky. It was a clear day with no clouds. The sound was an airplane that neither one of us could see because of its height in the sky—a first for two country boys, only accustomed to small engine or prop planes of the day.

A few years later when I was 11 or 12 years old visiting my Grandfather Raymon Smith, he had a Minneapolis Moline tractor with rubber tires and a tricycle front-end. He was disking and I wanted to help. He finally said that I could and he proceeded to show and tell me how to operate the hand clutch and throttle. When he thought I understood, he left to get the mules and started planting corn with the old horse-drawn planter.

I did very well until I got in the corner of the field and came too close to

Hal Smith farming at Kirksey

the fence. I stopped the tractor, but when I released the clutch, the front end of the tractor reared up and swung around, going over the fence. As I clutched the tractor it came down—but the front end was on one side of the fence and the rear end and disc were on the other and I was straddling the fence. I do not like to remember what Papa Smith said to me when he found me. However, we worked the rest of the day tearing down the fence, getting the tractor and disc back in the right field and putting the fence back up before we could go to the house for supper."

✼

Bettie Smith Stoll told of her early farm equipment experience:

Sam and Lois (Robinson) Brewer.

"Papa Brewer taught me how to drive, on the tractor. We would haul in hay with me on the tractor, Billy on the wagon, and Papa Brewer picking up the bales. But ... every time I was supposed to move forward a little, I would jerk the wagon and tractor letting out on the clutch, nearly throwing my brother off the wagon. Billy would fuss, but my grandfather would say, "Now Billy, she has to learn sometime."

Billy Dale Smith related to that story:
"The first time I drove a tractor, I was just 5 years old. I'd grown up on the farm, with my great-granddad, granddad and dad, but the biggest highlight was when I was about three foot tall, hauling hay at Papa Smith's farm. They needed an extra hand to drive the tractor, so they put me on the driver's seat. I could steer, but I couldn't reach the clutch without standing up. Daddy was picking up the hay bales and handing them onto the wagon where Papa Brewer was stacking. I don't remember much else because I was so focused on driving,

but I don't know to this day how Papa stayed on the wagon because I kept having to take my foot off the clutch to start and had to stand up to mash the clutch down to stop."

꿩꿩

Getting around got a whole lot easier as blacktopped roads inched their way toward the tiny farming community of Kirksey. The end of the horse and buggy days occurred somewhere around 1946, agriculture was improving due to more efficient farm machinery, and the days of using a mule to pull a plow were over. (The Kirksey Highway finally got blacktopped in the early 1950s.)

Smith family members were enthusiastic buyers as cars and pickup trucks became more common. Billy Smith recalled:

Reva, Geneva, Lois and Sam Brewer.

"I remember when Papa Brewer lived west of Mayfield he purchased a Plymouth that had a heater and radio on it. He refused to play the radio because he said it would run the battery down. He also would only use the heater when Mama Brewer or another female was in the car. If it was cold he told you to just put on more socks, clothes and another jacket—that's the way it was going to be.

My mother, Geneva Brewer Smith, said that when she and her sister, Reva, were 11 and 12 years old (approximately 1925), their father, Papa Brewer, bought a Model T or Model A Ford car for them to drive to school. It was one of the first cars in the Kirksey community and people would run to their windows to see it pass by. Mother, being the oldest at age 12, got to drive, and Aunt Reva would get in front of the car and turn the crank to start the engine as Mother sat in the seat and applied the gas to crank the car. Mother was a fast driver as well as being a good driver."

Billy Dale remembered Granny Smith talking about going up and down Backusburg Hill:

"The motor was in the front end with the gas on the firewall, in front of the wind shield. As it was higher than the motor, it would gravity flow to the engine. Pulling up a steep hill like the one at Backusburg, the motor would get higher than the gas tank and the car would die, so they had to go up hills backwards to keep them from running out of fuel."

Changes in Tobacco Farming

In mid-century, air-cured tobacco and burley tobacco came on the farm scene, varieties that were popular and commanded a good market price. The new crop was easier to grow because it didn't need to be suckered (the arduous process of pulling new growth off each tobacco plant) and there was no need for barn fires to smoke the tobacco because, being used in cigarettes, it did not need the finish that is required for snuff and chewing tobacco.

Herbicides, pesticides, and fertilizer also came into more prominent use. Billy Smith recalled:

"I remember when I was a young kid in the mid 1940s that I loved to stay on the farm with my grandpa. One year he had bought a 100-pound

Billy Smith holding fertilizer bag, with Papa Brewer.

bag of nitrate of soda (16 percent nitrogen). He was using a bucket and a tablespoon to fertilize each individual plant of tobacco by hand. Being a young kid I wanted to help, so he showed me how and then he took the old mule and began to plow the tobacco as I proceeded to put the fertilizer around each plant. I began to get tired and began putting a lot of fertilizer on each plant. The more I used the less heavy the bucket became. I got close to the end of the row and I really began to put the fertilizer around several plants.

In about three weeks, and after a couple good spring rains, there were a few rows and especially some plants at the end of the rows that were really growing and becoming quite a bit larger than any thing else in the field. Papa finally asked me one day if I knew anything about why those plants were so much larger. It took more than one time of questioning me before I told him what I had done. He was quite upset with me but he began to use fertilizer all the time after that."

Commercial greenhouses for tobacco plants.

In relating how tobacco production has changed, Billy Dale Smith said, "Today

most all tobacco plants are grown in greenhouses. In the early 1980s farmers started using greenhouses and waterbeds as a way to cut back on labor costs

Getting greenhouse plants to the setter.

from having to pull plants from beds. There is still a lot of labor involved with the greenhouse plants but it enables the farmer to do a lot of the work himself during a slow time of year for him. When setting time comes around in early May all he has to do after getting his ground ready is find help to ride the setter, a much easier job than pulling plants. Then, go to the greenhouse and load the plants to transplant them into the tobacco patch."

Setting, Topping, and Suckering

Josh Smith (far right) and local help prepare to set tobacco with greenhouse plants.

Billy Dale Smith with daughter Janae.

Setting tobacco does take practice and even the youngest in the family is taught how to ride the setter early in life. Billy Dale's daughter, Janae Smith, told of her personal experience:

"*The first time I rode the setter, Daddy drove real slow starting out, and I was doing great. Then he got to*

Billy Smith with son Billy Dale.

going faster, and I couldn't keep up with everyone else. I tried, but I missed getting several plants into the hole. So when he stopped the tractor, I had to get off and go back over the ground we'd just covered and fill up all the places I'd missed, using the tobacco peg."

꿔꿩

Topping or the breaking off of the plant occurred when the desired number of leaves had shaped. Mother Nature sent up new tops at the base of each leaf, providing the most painful labor known to mankind as the grower had to remove these "suckers" two to three times per season.

Luis Tapia topping tobacco at Smith Farms.

Additionally, there were times when large tobacco moths laid eggs on the leaves, and these had to be eradicated as well. These labor-intensive efforts of removal were known as suckering and worming tobacco.

In talking about the suckering process, Billy Dale shared this:

"Now I like to oil tobacco (treat it with a chemical compound) at the early button stage, before the flower blooms out. This seems to help control suckers better for me by getting them while they are small. We will also start topping the

Workers at Smith Farms suckering tobacco plants.

same day or next few days by cutting the tops out with pruning shears. This process happens at least two times per field. By cutting the tops out it allows the nutrients to go into the leaves on the tobacco plants instead of going into the flower. The plant flowers to reproduce and takes most of the nutrients and water for this process. That's why we top it. The suckers will then come out at each leaf where it connects to the stalk for another chance at putting another flower on to reproduce. That's why we burn the suckers off with oil."

Billy Dale's son, Josh Smith, told of his own experience with this part of the process:

Oiling tobacco at Smith Farms

"When I was a teenager, we were suckering and oiling down in Tennessee and we'd been down there all day. Those rows were so long you couldn't see the end until you were there. It's blistering hot, an hour or more away from home, there is no end in sight and you know you can't yet go home. The only thing you can pray for is rain, but because you're so far from home, you'd just have to wait it out, so you just keep working.

Well this particular day, it did rain so we took a break, and the leaves got muddy and messy from the splatters of the rain. As I was suckering that day, I'd worn shorts rather than jeans and when the rain stopped, the tobacco was wet and it was getting all this oil and chemical on my skin. Well, the nicotine was going through my body, though I wasn't aware of it. I began to feel bad about 4 p.m. and by the time I got home around 7 p.m., I took my shower and when I looked into the mirror I did not recognize myself. I was swollen, and my skin color was bright red. I'm sure I had either nicotine or chemical poisoning, but the next day, I had to go back to the patch because all the swelling was gone."

Cutting

Cutting and spiking tobacco at Smith Farms.

Cutting time typically arrives in September after the giant leaves reach down nearly to the ground, as they are ripe. Neighborhood crews shared in the cutting process, swapping labor to house the tobacco for the firing process where the plant is cured for market. In the 1980s local labor became so hard to find that the Smiths were forced to bring in migrant labor to work in the tobacco fields.

Billy Dale told about the last year his dad had a tobacco crop:

"It was in the middle of today's farm; he had a good sized crew working that day. They split and then hung the tobacco. I wasn't really big enough to split it as I wasn't as tall as the plants. The men were all on one side of the field where they couldn't see me. I began cutting the tobacco where they couldn't see me. They worked around me, and a man that was working for Dad told him that some of the tobacco hadn't been split. I was really worried that I was going to get in trouble. I didn't—but Daddy probably knew who had cut the plants and left them lying."

Workers place the cut tobacco on the scaffold wagons at Smith Farms.

Josh chimed in:

"I remember my first tobacco crop when I was too little to cut tobacco. Dad told me that if I wanted to make some money that I could pick up leaves as they went through cutting, spiking and putting it on the wagon. When my arms were full, I was to take them to the wagon, and put them in the shade where it wouldn't get burned by the sun.

Dad told me that I was the slowest he'd ever seen. It was hot and I was little, so of course I didn't work too hard. He told me I should think of every leaf as a dollar bill, trying to encourage me along. Granny Smith came out later in the evening with rubber bands to help me tie the leaves up. We took the leaves back to the shop and she tied them and then put them on a stick, explaining how this process was to work.

Well, I was just a little kid and for weeks after picking up all those leaves, I kept thinking about what Dad said, that each one was worth a dollar, so I'm anticipating getting about $500 because I'm sure I picked up that many. A few months later, when most any child would have long forgotten about those leaves, I was asking daddy every day about my share of the leaves. I finally got a check for $101, which for a young boy, was good money."

Preparing for Market

Once the tobacco is cut and spiked, it is housed or hung in the barn. Billy Dale shares one of his earliest memories of this part of the process:

"The first barn where I worked in housing tobacco was at Papa Smith's farm. They put me up in the top of the barn to hang tobacco

Billy Dale Smith with dad, Billy, taking tobacco from the barn for stripping.

as it was handed up to the top tiers. I was somewhere around 8 or 10 and my legs could just barely reach across the tier poles. The barn at Papa Smith's farm is still in use today for this same purpose."

As the curing process comes to an end, often warm rain provided seasonable weather to bring the tobacco "in order." Preparing the tobacco for sale included stripping the prime leaves and lugs—the bottom most leaves—and tying them together by hand. Once prepared for market, the family would deliver the crop on into March of the following year.

According to Josh Smith:

"The way we strip tobacco now is so different than we used to. When Granny and Hal were living, they'd invite their retired friends to come help us strip. The younger adults would take the lugs off at the wagon, then throw the leaves on a table, and stand there on concrete floors, stripping the leaves."

The senior citizens would sit in chairs and strip at their own pace, talking all day about their grandkids, family members and neighbors. They'd have a big time catching up with one another, passing the day away. Instead of just throwing the tied leaves in a box, they had to take each leaf and collect them into a handful, then tie them up."

Billy Dale stripping tobacco with Granny (Geneva Brewer) Smith to his left.

Billy Dale explained:

"Hand tying normally included eight to ten leaves to a hand. After tying a pile of hand-tied tobacco, you would have to book it down. This would require you to straighten it out long ways—with the heads together—in a pile or on a wagon. Then it would be taken to market the

same way. Sometimes two hands at a time at each process all the way to the basket on the tobacco floor where it was sold."

Josh continued:

"Now we have a line of people, with a conveyor belt with a chain and motor on the back. The tobacco stalk is on a stick and as it comes in, you take it off the wagon and put it on the conveyor belt. Once it is on the belt, it starts through the stripping line. Each person in the line has a different job. At the beginning, the lugs and trash come off, leaving only the best leaves. The people in the back of the line take off the good leaves and put them in a box for shipping. The boxes weigh hundreds of pounds. The productivity of tobacco has picked up so much with these changes in the production process, even in my lifetime. Hopefully it will get even easier as time goes by."

Boxed tobacco ready for shipping to market.

Billy Dale commented:

"It has become easier in recent years. We started boxing tobacco in bales where we could place a layer at a time onto a basket. Today we just put the tobacco into big cardboard boxes tie the box, load it on a truck and haul it to the tobacco company."

Sending tobacco to market, the old fashioned way, with horse and wagon.
Photo courtesy Kentucky Historical Society.

Said Josh:

"Yeah, Dad actually made me believe that I was the best boxer in the world. When I was a little kid, I thought he wanted me to be the one

to do the boxing, making it look as perfect as I could. Come to find out, I was the smallest in the group, so I fit inside the box the easiest, so that became my job. But he always made me feel like I was his guy and that I knew how to do it just right. I actually enjoyed boxing tobacco, so I guess he had the right strategy and the right job for me."

Selling

Buyers of tobacco in the late 1800s and early 1900s would look over the leaf in the barn during the winter and haggle with the farmer for his crop. Upon agreement, a contract was signed for delivery. Over time, farmers began to feel that a competitive market was more desirable. A chute was built in the county seat of Murray where growers could bring their tobacco in bulk and sell to buyers.

Buyers at the chute would bid on the crops. There were times when the bidding was rigged to the disadvantage of the farmers because of an understanding between the buyers. However, the farmer had little alternative but to sell at whatever price he was offered for the next year's income. Almost a full year's worth of work in a crop yielded only a meager amount of revenue for the family.

Burley tobacco being housed in curing barn.

Today, the eighth and ninth generations of Smiths are using computer technology to assist their farming operations. As Billy Smith noted:

"Most modern agricultural equipment now has GPS guidance systems. As you cross the field a computer provides on-the-go readouts. In the winter months the fertilizer dealer or farmer will use the GPS guidance systems to conduct soil tests in each two-and-a-half-acre plot.

The computer tells the truck what mix of fertilizer and how much to put on the ground. A good example is the new combines with computers which can tell you on-the-go how much the yield of each crop is anywhere in the field, moisture content, yield per acre, total yield per field and total yield for each farm within 1 percent of scaled weights. There is new technology every day—you have to run to keep up."

❧❧

As the Smith family's primary cash crop, tobacco was the agricultural focal point over the years. Here is a closer look at "Tobacco: Then and Now," based on Billy Smith's recollections and *The Story of Calloway County*, a local history.

The Great Depression continued the downward push in tobacco prices that began earlier in the century. The *Story of Calloway County* indicates that the market deterioration persisted in 1912 despite the efforts of the Planters Protective Association that had begun eight years earlier. With only 35 percent of the district's total crop under the association's control, it became clear that government intervention was needed to lift farmers out of their despair.

Billy Smith explained:

"Sometime after the Depression, during the Franklin D. Roosevelt administration, the U.S. government's farm program was established. The program established a federal government grading system to assess tobacco

quality, issuing grade cards defining different quality and price levels and then grading each farmer's tobacco as it was readied for market. Each tobacco-producing region was required to form its own association, or cooperative, to buy farmers' tobacco at

Ready for market in 2009.

a guaranteed price when the commercial buyers' bids were too low during the warehouse auction or they refused to pay the government-graded price. Farmers would receive checks from the government, and the associations would process the tobacco and hold it until it could be sold to local, national or international buyers at a profit. Tobacco that was purchased by the association, or co-op, was referred to as going to the "pool." The program worked well for 30 to 40 years, giving farmers a reliable bottom-line income regardless of the tobacco companies' bids."

The *Story of Calloway County* stated, "In 1948 the Kentucky state legislature enacted farm-to-market highway legislation, and that created the change in how farm operations would work. As the years rolled on by, other changes on the farm occurred. In 1950 the man who had patented the tobacco sprayer, the tobacco hoe and other farm tools died, Crawford Duncan Holt, a local horticulturist and inventor. Mr. Holt was well known for his newspaper articles and prior to his death he warned of the ultimate effects of the allotment system based on production history with no regard for family needs. He predicted that the system would virtually wipe out most small farms within

Smoking barns at Smith Farms.

Early tobacco.

20 years. The high cost of mechanization on the farm was also considered a contributing factor."

The historical work also pointed out that, "Tobacco was no longer king of the farm in Calloway County; however it was something like royalty when 9 million pounds were sold for an average of $41.67 per pound by March 3, 1961, a record despite the generally depressed business condition over the nation. Growers voiced no hesitancy in voting approval of tobacco quotas in the regular three-year referendum on February 24, a control method devised by the U.S. Department of Agriculture to keep supply more in harmony with demand yet create a controlled scarcity to sustain higher prices—a practice of ultimate self destruction for Calloway farmers on world markets."

The quota system could not be changed without the vote of the quota owner. The growers pushed Congress to do something to change the government program. This was all occurring at the same time that people in the U.S. began to raise questions about health issues with smoking and other use of tobacco.

It took nearly 50 years for Holt's prediction to come true (that the system would wipe out farms), but it finally happened in the 1990s. As the federal government continued to tighten production controls to limit the growth of the surplus, which was already huge, the acreage allotments were reduced for tobacco farmers while the price per pound was increased to keep pace with inflation.

Senators from tobacco-producing states led the effort to develop a buyout program for tobacco farmers. With small acreage allotments, many farmers could not rent or lease enough acres to be profitable and frequently had to drive up to 20 or 30 miles to get enough acreage to survive. The costs were simply too great.

With the buyout program, farmers could continue to raise as much tobacco as they wanted, but the government price supports were gone. The small and less efficient farmers could not survive. This is why tobacco today is grown on fewer farms with larger acreage. A farmer must have a contract with a buyer before he starts a crop or he could wind up with no market for his crop or a price that would bankrupt him.

The quota owner got his base paid for and the grower got the money that was left in the tobacco associations that were owned by the grower. This is what was called the tobacco buyout program, initiated in 2004 and to be paid for over a 10-year period.

Tobacco barn in Kirksey Community. *Photo dated 2010.*

Billy Smith recalled:

"The U.S. government made farmers join the association by charging them a small membership fee to participate. The fee was somewhere around $7.50 to join the association and it was a one-time fee. When the tobacco buyout occurred in 2004, the local associations had to sell their stocks as well as the facilities they owned. The tobacco program never cost the government any money as it was self-sufficient. As the buyout proceeded and the local associations sold their inventory and facilities, the tobacco program was over. The tobacco buyout came from funds assessed from manufacturers and importers of all of tobacco products sold in the United States. This is estimated to total $10.14 billion over a ten year period. This program was co-sponsored by Kentucky U.S. Sen. Mitch McConnell."

An unexpected result of the program was the increase in the price of farmland in west Kentucky and west Tennessee to more than $4,000 an acre from $2,000 an acre the year before. The primary reason for this was the fact that farmers would be receiving a set amount of buyout money with the demise of the tobacco program.

Billy Smith looked to the future:

"I believe that in the next 10 to 15 years the tobacco producer will have over-produced and they will have to reduce their acreage and/or poundage. There is one ray of hope that farmers have, and that is in the use of tobacco as medicine. There is a company in Owensboro, Ky., that says it has found a gene in tobacco that has potential in the medical field, and this potential opportunity could save the tobacco industry for several more years."

Like everything else today, consolidation is king and buyers are few and far between. Just in the first decade of the 21st century, Phillip Morris Tobacco Company bought out the U.S. Tobacco Company, and in 2007, Con Wood was purchased by R. J. Reynolds Tobacco Company.

For the past 100 years or so, tobacco was grown by the family and the acreage was governed by the number of children in the family.

Billy continued:

"Over the years, we went from neighbors swapping work to the farmer hiring local help, and now we are using migrant workers, furnishing their housing, transportation and travel expenses to and from Mexico. While wages vary from year to year, in 2008 they were about $10 per hour with fringe benefits, bringing the total to somewhere in the $13 to $14 per hour range."

Since the 1990s dark fired tobacco has become more popular because it is being used as a smokeless tobacco and today is selling for about 25 percent premium above other tobaccos. It is being exported all over the world. It takes a special knowledge and know-how to fire and finish this kind of tobacco. It is a process that is passed down from one generation to another—from father to son—and has been in the Smith family over the last 150 years.

CHAPTER V

Transportation

Railroads

*R*eflecting on the use of railroads for agricultural transportation, Billy Smith noted:

"The railroads were the cheapest and most reliable form of long distant travel in the first half of the 20th century. The first time that Shirley and I went to Chicago, we went to Fulton, Ky., to the passenger depot and caught the train there to Chicago. It ran from Chicago to New Orleans every day, with one train going north and another going south. Speaking of Fulton, it was considered halfway between New Orleans and Chicago. There was

an icing house in Fulton and the trains would stop there to re-ice the bananas for the rest of the trip to Chicago, and on to Minneapolis, Mn. That is the reason that Fulton has the Banana Festival each year.

When Shirley and I traveled to the west coast several times after I retired, I was surprised to see lots of trains in the middle of the country and out in the west. The trains were

Old train, *photo courtesy William (Bill) Hamilton Bryant, Jr.'s family.*

hauling piggyback trailers from the west coast into the Midwest and from New Orleans to the upper Midwest. Also, lots of coal from the west coast, potash out of Canada as well as petroleum products were being moved by unit trains of 60 to 100 rail cars in one unit. With dedicated cargo and destinations, the trains have gotten back some of their business."

Trains were used extensively in the mid 1940s to enhance the war effort by moving materials and equipment across the county as well as serving as the primary transportation for soldiers.

Cooper's Warehouse in Christian County, Ky., showing process of sampling dark tobacco out of hogsheads, pronounced "hogszits." *Photo courtesy William T. Turner, Christian County Historian*

The use of passenger trains began waning by 1966, even though cargo of all types was still in transit. Even the famous Dixie Flyer, the crack train of the Louisville & Nashville Railroad, made its farewell run. Trains no longer stopped in the smaller towns where it was a matter of course in bygone years to "meet the train." (*Kentucky: Land of Contrast*)

Trucks, Four-Wheelers and Gators

Billy Smith recalls:

"In the1970s the trucking industry started to take over a lot of the freight hauling that the trains were doing. The tobacco industry was one industry that dropped out of using water transportation and began using the rail system and eventually the trucking industry to move their products. Dark fired tobacco for export originally was shipped by water to New Orleans. but by the '40s and '50s they started using the railroad to get tobacco to New Orleans.

When I worked at Hutson Chemical Company, we used to load train cars with tobacco hogsheads for export out of New Orleans. With the to-bacco buyout and the demise of the Western Tobacco Warehouse Associa-

Billy Smith with the Hutson Chemical Company truck.

tion, there is no longer any tobacco processed in Murray and no more tobacco stored in west Kentucky.

When plane fares got cheap, especially when Southwest Airlines and others came into the picture, train rides went the way of Greyhound Bus travel—it declined. Most everyone wanted to go fast and get to their destination in a few hours instead of on an overnight trip. Train travel in the '30s, '40s, and '50s was for the wealthy people who had time and money to travel. Travelers eventually got into a big hurry and did not have time to waste. Cheap airfare and coast-to-coast air service probably did more to do away with passenger train service than any other thing."

꿍꿍

Billy Dale Smith has always loved trucks and shared this story about one of his first trucks:

"At Hal's farm one winter, I was about 16 years old and I'd bought a 1973 four-wheel drive pickup truck. Everybody liked to go mudding. I

Billy Dale's pick-up truck 1988.

didn't want to go on anyone else's farm, so I went to Hal's farm. By then it was my responsibility to keep it up, clean it, etc. I didn't ask permission, just went out there and made a race track. Well, Hal thought I'd made a damn mess. I don't think he ever said too much to me other than asking me why I had done it. The next year I had to disk up the mess and plant it and you could never tell that there had been a mess, but it really looked bad all winter."

Upon hearing his father's story, Josh Smith noted:

"Sure wished I'd known about that! When I was a kid, Dad had a four-wheeler and I used to ride it for fun in the woods close by our house. There were several trails in the woods as well as all over the farm. This four-wheeler was one of those heavy duty machines, the kind that are used for hauling stuff around. I loved to jump over things and go through the creek, all the things that boys like to do, though I knew I probably shouldn't.

I'd drive through the creek at the back of the farm, over on the Cain place behind our house. One day I was trying to figure out the paths going from field to field, but as I was young, I didn't understand how they all met up. Come to find out, there is not one path that goes all the way through the farm. I didn't want to go around by the road as it would take too long,

so I went down the middle path, thinking that it would take me closer to where I was supposed to be, but it didn't connect back to the creek as I'd thought it would. So, I pulled a big U-turn out into dad's

Billy Dale pulling Josh on the 4-wheeler.

bean crop. Now, it wasn't full-grown beans, but they were up, just hadn't turned yet. Well, I knocked down a good portion of it where I had made the turn.

This was probably done on a Saturday while I was out of school. In a few days, Dad came to me one afternoon and said, 'I see you've been riding your four-wheeler.' I told him I hadn't, but he knew it had to be me as he and I were the only ones who ever drove it. So, he took me over to where I'd turned around and of course what I had done was very noticeable. I thought I was too old for a whipping at that time, but I was wrong. I got a few good licks for this one….sure wish I'd known about what you did at Hal's!"

In defending himself, Billy Dale said:

"I soon found out that I could tear up enough, just by farming, that I didn't have to get out in the mud to do so. It is fun to go four-wheeling, but I get as much of it as I want now."

Janae Smith recalled the time when her grandfather Smith (Billy) took her for a ride:

"When Pap first bought his Gator, we went riding in the snow and got stuck in a ditch. He didn't have his cell phone, so he couldn't call anyone to come help us. We kept trying to get out on our own, but it wouldn't budge. We were dressed in our overalls and had on our thermal underwear, and it was a good thing as we were out there about two hours and ended up having to walk back to the house."

Janae Smith in Pap's Gator.

Air Travel

Surprising as it may seem, airplanes were among the other forms of transportation available in Calloway County. Granted, the planes were small. But in 1961 an airport was built on 146 acres northwest of Murray in the Penny community, a project considered essential for industrial development.

The 3,500-foot airstrip was financed with federal and local funds and was named for Verne Kyle, Murray Manufacturing plant manager, whose daughter was a schoolmate of Shirley Smith.

Murray Calloway County Airport, *photo courtesy Hutson Chemical Company brochure.*

Billy Smith remembered his time management challenges after going to work Hutson Chemical in 1960:

"I continued to farm some, and we were also very active in Farm Bureau as I had become a state director. Having to travel to Louisville several times a year, it was taking two to three days to attend a meeting and it was taking too much time away from work at Hutson's. I began having Toy Lenin or Jan Shot fly me to meetings in Louisville in a Cessna plane. I began to love flying at low altitudes, being able to see the crops below me. They would let me take the controls from time to time, and I just thought it would be nice to learn to fly myself.

Crop dusting plane over barn in Calloway County.

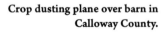

I started taking lessons at the local airport and soon was able to fly myself around the general area. I got up to a little over 200 hours of flight time and suddenly, Stub Wilson, who was older than I and a good friend, was killed in a plane crash in Gadsden, Alabama. Then just a few weeks later Toy Lenin got killed as he was trying to find the Crossville, Tennessee airport in bad weather. This really brought me to my knees and reminded me that I could get killed as well. I had taken each of our children up for a plane ride, and this made Shirley very nervous. I was busy with work, Farm Bureau, and trying to farm as well, and flying left me little time to farm so I decided to give up flying myself as I did not respect the weather and when I wanted to go I did not like to hear that I could not fly. I was always pushing Toy or Jan to go when the weather was bad. I remember one time Toy flew us to Louisville by flying low up the Ohio River until we got to Louisville. I thought it was probably a good time to quit.

While I was working for Hutson's, Mr. Hutson bought a jet ranger helicopter. As I was vice president of the company, I had second call on the craft and got to fly more than I wanted to. He soon purchased a twin engine Piper Navaho that was certified for flying in bad weather and we had lots of time in it. I was in it once when we lost an engine and had to make an emergency landing at Baton Rouge, La.

Woody Herndon with Hutson's helicopter, *photo courtesy Hutson Chemical Company brochure.*

Another time we were on our way home from Greenville, Miss., and one of the motors quit and we made our landing at Murray airport on one engine. I quit flying in the Piper Navaho after that and Mr. Hutson sold that plane."

Billy Smith at Hutson's in the 1980s.

Josh has a particular memory:

"I've always thought Pap (Billy Smith) was Superman. One time when I was little, I was walking from my house to their house, and because I watched Miami Vice on TV at that time, I knew what helicopters were. One day I saw Pap running out of his house with his hat on, waving goodbye to me. He was getting into a helicopter that was landing in their back yard. In my head, I was thinking he was a Secret Service guy or something of that nature, but I learned as I got older that it was just Woody, picking him up to go to work."

CHAPTER VI

The Importance of Education

From the one-room schoolhouses of the early years to the modern facilities of today, the Smith family has valued education—and remembered rich stories from their experiences—through the generations.

The Kentucky Constitution requires that education be provided, and early legislation mandated that each county set aside land and provide free public schools, at least one of which had to be within walking distance for every student. *The Story of Calloway County* tells us that schools were available for the most part in rural areas as early as the Civil War, and Moonlight Schools were created to combat illiteracy.

But early schooling was a struggle. Dr. Thomas Clark notes in *Agrarian Kentucky* that, "teaching in Kentucky country schools prior to 1930 often required the wit of Solomon, the courage of David, the fortitude of Job and the self-sacrifice of the widow and her mite. 'Keeping' school was as much a test of physical self-endurance as of intellectual competence and many a teacher proved to have neither. Even the best teachers were inadequately prepared and prior to 1908 had no place to turn for training."

❦

Our Granny, Geneva Smith, enjoyed talking about her days at the Little Rock School. She also told stories about her parents attending the Harding School. Students got an early start in those days, often doing their morning chores before coming to school. Geneva and her sister, Reva, would have walked to school, returning home to complete their evening chores at the end of the day.

Harding School, Lois Robinson Brewer is the fourth from the right, bottom row.

A Photographic Potpourri of Calloway County indicates that most one-room school buildings of that day were solidly built structures with sparse furnishings that included such necessities as benches or school desks, blackboards, an eraser and a scant supply of chalk. Most were heated with a pot-bellied stove, and a galvanized bucket with a shared drinking cup was always available. Another amenity was the standard outhouse, typically of the two- or three-hole variety.

One-room schools began to disappear as roads improved. The consolidation of schools provided better opportunities and expanded curricula. But the one-room Little Rock School was transformational for the Kirksey community, as well as the entire county, because of the vision of the lone teacher employed there.

In researching our Smith family materials we came across a faded 1929 publication called *The Pathfinder* published by the senior class of the Kirksey High School (formerly known as the Calloway County Normal

**1929 KHS Pathfinder, Kirksey
High School newsletter.**

College)—the first graduating class of the
newly named school.

The Pathfinder featured an historic
account of the early days of education in the
Kirksey community:

> *"In the early Autumn of 1899, there
> originated in the mind of a young school
> teacher, living in the little village of Kirksey
> and teaching at a nearby rural school, Little
> Rock, an idea to establish a school district
> in the Kirksey community and to build in*
> *that district a school building which was to be of magnificent proportions.
> … This man who conceived the idea of better schooling facilities for the
> Kirksey community and who carried out his idea with the same tireless
> energy that has characterized his life, is none other than Calloway
> County's own illustrious son, Rainey T. Wells, who is today president of
> Murray State Teachers College."*

We were also delighted to learn that one of the professors teaching at
the school and named within the article was Bert Smith, one of our distant
cousins.

A 1929 summer issue of a monthly newsletter titled the Kirksey High
School *Echo* issued a welcome to all the students from Little Rock and
Corinth, who would be joining them for the fall semester: "We look forward
with an eager anticipation of the pleasant associations that we shall have with
you. We believe that you are going to enjoy becoming a part of our school
and we are going to do our best to initiate you into the fullest participation of
every opportunity and benefit that is ours as a school."

In 1907 a wonderful advertisement promoted the new school: "Room
and board at Kirksey only $8. … The best people you ever ate and slept
with."

The Calloway County Normal College continued from 1899 until 1913 when it became a standard two-year high school. The demand for an additional year of high school classes and a growing number of students prompted a decision to build a new brick structure, with new electrical amenities.

In 1923 the school was renamed Kirksey High School, which had shared space on the campus and took over the entire facility as a four-year high school. Kirksey High School remained until 1960, when the county schools merged into one system. Bettie Smith Stoll, sister of Billy Smith, was a senior in the last graduating class of Kirksey High School, which became an elementary school until 1975. Then, the property was sold to the Kirksey United Methodist Church.

Kirksey High School, *courtesy The Eagle, 1954 KHS Annual.*

The Echo was marketed as a monthly publication created by students and was sold by subscription to county residents for 50 cents a year. Our Granddaddy Hal Smith was news editor of this publication during his senior year of 1929-1930. An entry from his junior year reads: "Hal, better known as 'Al' Smith, is a new man but not at all a bad one. He matched well against any center anywhere for his 'age.' He proved himself a capable player by playing in any position on the team."

Hal, aka "Al," wrote several articles in the *Echo* (included below) and served as vice president of his junior class. He was captain of the basketball team in 1929 and 1930, and appeared in two plays, *Go Slow Mary*, and *He's My Pal*. He served as

Hal Smith, center front, and the basketball team at Kirksey High School, 1929-30.

president of the Wilsonian Society and managed to make the honor roll. Hal graduated from Kirksey High School in 1930 and went for additional studies at Draughn's Business College in Paducah.

SCHOOL NEWS, BY HAL SMITH
OCTOBER 1930

Hal Smith, KHS graduation photo, 1930.

Kirksey has been a pretty lively place for the past several weeks. Things have been happening around this school. There wasn't much said about it, but the Eagles did a man-sized job about two weeks ago. They made a trip over to Lynn Grove and drove the "Yaller Wildcats" out of their dens. It was a bad night, too, and they howled something awful, but they couldn't help themselves. The team hasn't got all the cat-hair picked out of their feathers yet.

And, by the way, did you know that the Kirksey agricultural boys have raised, stripped and have ready for market over a thousand sticks of tobacco? Well, it's a "fack" as Uncle Ben says. We'll soon have some money around this place. Maybe we can pay the taxes.

I want to tell you about the meeting, too. You know the Methodist congregation have just got through constructing a new church adjoining the school ground and they held their first meeting the first week in December. The weatherman said he wasn't going to let it be a success, but you know, that bunch just took things into their own hands and put it over big. We went over on several occasions and we all acknowledge that we feel a right smart better for it.

And listen, fellers, let's all get together and make this place around here a newsy one so I won't have to think so much the next time I write the news. That's all. Hope you all have a Merry Christmas and a Happy New Year. *Al*

DON'T GIVE UP THE SHIP, BY HAL SMITH
OCTOBER 30, 1930

Due to the fact that we have not had any rain this summer, you can easily look about you and find farmers that seem to be willing to give up the idea of farming as their life's vocation. I will admit that we haven't had any season this summer, and there has not been scarcely any feedstuff made, and the tobacco crop in most localities is completely a failure. But farmers I want to ask you a question, "How many years in twenty-five do we have like the one we have just experienced?

Don't sell your cattle and livestock for nothing if you can possibly get them through till grass comes again next spring.

The corn that is standing in the fields with not even a shoot on it is almost equal to red top hay in feeding value if it is cut at the right time, and cured out properly. The fall sowing of rye, oats and wheat for early spring pasture will help a great deal in solving the problem that most farmers throughout the country are confronted with, and I ask you again, why give up all hopes? There is never anything so bad but what it could have been worse.

❧❧

Hal's son, William Hal (Billy) Smith, Jr., graduated from Kirksey High in 1955 and served as senior class reporter and president of the Kirksey Future Farmers of America. Billy recalled his early days at the Mayfield elementary school:

"I started to grade school at Lee School in Mayfield and walked several blocks to school every day. When I was 6 years old, which was the fall of

William (Billy) Hal Smith, Jr. Kirksey High School Graduation 1955.

1943, times were hard, and I remember that I got one new pair of shoes each year. They became my Sunday shoes, and last year's new shoes became my everyday shoes. Each year when school started, mother would buy me seven new white short sleeve under shirts and two or three pairs of blue jeans. I wore them to school my first eight years, blue jeans and white tee shirts. I made a decision if I ever had any money that I would never wear blue jeans again. I did not buy a pair of blue jeans until I turned 70 years old and now I own two pair, probably the only ones I will ever have. I just don't like them all that much.

Times were hard in the '40s, and Mother would always buy my dress clothes just one size too big. That way I could wear them that year and the next year they would be about the right size, and most of the times I could wear them on into the third year. I always tried to outgrow them so I could get new ones. The pants that I hated wearing the most were a pair of knickers. We had paper drives and clothing drives to help with the war effort, and this was a big deal for a small young kid."

Billy Smith in pair of knickers that he hated. Great hat too.

Billy wasn't the only elementary school student helping with the war. According to *Recollections of Calloway County*, the Utterback School in Calloway County was recognized for its efforts to collect scrap iron for the war during 1942. Even though the school only had 23 students, they collected more scrap iron per capita in a statewide, month-long drive than any other school of any size in the state.

Billy remembered:

"I went to middle school in Mayfield, I played football, and tried to learn to play the tuba or base horn. I could not march in step. When I was in the 7th grade I also had sliders disease. This is caused when the little

bone just below the kneecap does not attach itself to the shinbone, and I had to wear a cast on both legs for six weeks so the bone would attach itself. They said that riding a bicycle caused this problem. Dad had to buy me a motor scooter to ride to school as my bicycle riding was over. Mother and Dad did not have time to deliver me to school and pick me up because of working at the store.

Linnie Brewer with brothers Sam and Clay.

Our Aunt Linnie, Papa Brewer's sister, was a history teacher at Mayfield Middle School, and I liked history. Daddy had her as a teacher when he was in school, too. I remember that I had to keep a notebook, the first time I had to do it I got a D, and I was so mad—she said she couldn't read it. I was determined to do better the next time, so I worked real hard, wrote it real neat, turned it in and she gave me a D again. When I asked her why, she said she didn't think I'd done it, that I'd gotten someone else to do it. She gave me the worst grade I ever got my entire time in school—I will never forget, or forgive her for that."

☙❧

Reflecting on his education in farm management as well as life, Billy recalled:

"We were going to the annual FFA convention in Louisville, and this was the trip where I learned to eat out in a big city. Our Ag teacher, Harvey Ellis, carried us to the Blue Boar Cafeteria. This was the first trip for us boys to a big city, and the Blue Boar Cafeteria had more food on display to eat than any of us had ever seen in one place. We started down the buffet line and filled our trays 'til they were so full that we could not put any thing

Harvey Ellis, Ag teacher at Kirksey High School.
Photo courtesy The Eagle, 1954 KHS Annual

else on them. When we went through the checkout lane were we ever surprised at the cost of food in Louisville. Most of us barely had enough money to pay our bill. Harvey

Post card of the Blue Boar Cafeteria interior.

finally stepped in and paid for our dinner that day; I sure hope he had an expense account. This was a great experience for teenage boys in a big city for their first time."

Mr. Ellis submitted this announcement about the Louisville trip to the *Murray Ledger and Times*:

"In 1954 at the Kentucky State Fair held in Louisville, the Kirksey Future Farmers of America delegation swept the market clean with 37 cash awards in the Green Tobacco division, the second year in a row for the chapter to lead the state."

᛭

Many rural Kentucky schools were ill-equipped, lacking both appropriate books and qualified teachers. In 1949, the Kentucky legislature addressed the inadequacies and mandated equal funding for all schools. In the early 1960s Billy and Shirley's children, Billy Dale and Bobbie, attended Kirksey when it was an elementary school.

To work on improving education quality, Shirley Smith recalled:

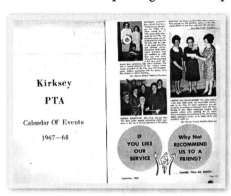

Shirley Smith shown in PTA newsletter for her work on safety issues in Murray.

"*I ran for the PTA president when Bobbie and Billy Dale were in the first and second or second and third grade, and was elected. The second grade teacher was not a board certified teacher, as we found out when our son, Billy Dale, was in her class. Several of our friends who had children in that class rationalized that we had to do something about it to get her out, or our children's education would suffer. We then got Lubie Parrish to run for school board member and he won. Then we went to work on ousting the superintendent of Calloway County Schools. We had lots of strategy meetings at night with the Ray Broach family, Max Hurt's family, Lubie and Reba Parrish and several other parents of Kirksey school kids. We thought at that time that we might help get something done immediately.*

Since I had attended and graduated from the Murray City School system we were familiar with their programming and reasoned that the city's educational system was, at the time, the better of the two systems. It offered a much bigger and more advanced curriculum. As I was already working at the Murray State University bookstore, and granddaddy Hal was working in the same building, it would be much more convenient for us to send the kids to the city school system. Howard and Sue Bazzell, our neighbors, were already sending their son, Charlie, to the

Bobbie Smith Bryant shown with neighbor and childhood friend, Charlie Bazzell. *Photo taken at their piano recital in the 1960s.*

city system, and they talked with us and assured us that he was receiving a
better education and that was why they were sending him there.

PRESIDENT'S CALENDAR

1967-1968

Kentucky Congress of Parents and Teachers

Shirley Smith's PTA calendar
for 1967-68.

*After talking to Howard and Sue
and many others, we made the switch to
the city system. I would leave at 8 a.m.
taking Charlie, Billy Dale and Bobbie
to school in the mornings on my way to
work. Sue would pick the three children
up at 3:10 p.m. and take Billy Dale
and Bobbie to MSU where Hal worked,
and when I got off work at 4:30 p.m., I
would pick up the kids and come home.
Hal seemed to enjoy watching the
kids as he was the keeper of the pool*
*room and Billy Dale and Bobbie had a chance to play pool, watch television
or get their homework finished. This was not particularly educational, but
it was safe, got the job done and we were satisfied that we were doing the
right thing for their education.*

*With my work at the MSU bookstore, keeping house, raising two
kids and keeping them in clean clothes, and seeing after their dad, I had
my hands full. I found it was a good thing that I didn't have any more
PTA'ing after that!"*

❧

The Kirksey School, in all its
iterations, was an important piece of the
community's culture, recognized with
an historic marker in 1994. The day the
marker was placed at the former site of
the school, Rainey Wells' grandson,
Wells Lovett, remarked: "If there had

Calloway County Normal College
(precursor to Murray State University),
historic marker located in Kirksey.

never been a Calloway Normal College, Murray State University would never have happened." With help and $117,000 from more than 1,000 residents, Dr. Wells planned, organized and founded Murray State Normal School in 1923 and it was opened to teach students to become professional teachers. The name of the school changed a number of times through the years until, in 1966, it became Murray State University.

❦

Education has always been a priority for the Smith family. In addition to Aunt Linnie, several family members have been educators in Calloway County. Bert Smith, one of Henry Smith's grandsons, was listed as professor of the 8th grade at Murray High School in 1910 and was a professor at the Calloway Normal College in 1929. In the 1938 yearbook, Haleene Smith is listed as faculty at Kirksey High School. She and her sister, Delle Smith, daughters of James Franklin Smith, taught for many years in the Calloway County system. In 1964, the *Murray Ledger & Times* noted that a unique level of recognition was bestowed upon Haleene Smith and several other teachers for their 30-year tenure.

Haleene Smith, 3rd grade teacher at Kirksey for over 30 years. She was one of the daughters of James Franklin Smith and a sister to Raymon Smith. *Photo courtesy The Eagle, 1954 KHS Annual*

Billy Dale Smith remembered Aunt Haleene as his third grade teacher:

"I was her teacher's pet. She had so many knot-heads in her class, I guess I was her favorite. I just remember her being a great big, tall woman, kind and gentle, she was a pretty good ole gal."

❦

Bettie Smith, Billy's sister and Hal's daughter, taught for 27 years in the McCracken County school system and continued working as a substitute teacher 14 years after retirement. Bobbie Smith Bryant recalled a scary situation

Bettie Smith Stoll, pianist.

that involved her Aunt Bettie, who was a music teacher:

"One year at Christmas I went with Granny and Hal over to Paducah to watch Aunt Bettie lead her choir in a Christmas pageant. The music was very pretty and what I was most excited about was when they lowered the lights and everyone in the choir held a lit candle as they sang Silent Night.

Each member of the choir had on a white choir robe with blue or black bow ties. One of the young boys accidentally set the robe in front of him on fire with his candle. Amazingly enough, the student with the flaming robe was able to pull it over his head and put out the fire. Everyone kept right on singing as though nothing had happened. I was mighty impressed with Aunt Bettie and her students that day!"

Education continues to be part of the Smith family heritage as Josh Smith, son of current Smith Farms owner Billy Dale Smith, is a middle school teacher at Calloway County Middle School. His wife, Melissa (Missy) Jenkins Smith, is also a teacher.

Missy Jenkins Smith shown with Kentucky State Representative Brad Montell while speaking at schools in Shelby County.

Josh Smith coaching his students at Calloway County Middle school, 2010.

CHAPTER VII

Harrowing Moments on the Farm

O f all the animals raised on Kentucky's farms, the hog has been the most self sufficient, according to *Kentucky Encyclopedia,* and has supplied many a dinner table with delectable meals in addition to lard and seasonings. Hogs also have played a role in some entertaining stories.

Bobbie Smith Bryant remembered well the day she and her family were at a neighbor's house where the adults were stripping tobacco:

Dovie Sutherland Brewer feeding her pigs.

"Billy Dale and I were among several children playing outside at Monice McCallon's place. We were playing tag and lots of other games and suddenly decided it would be more fun to chase their new litter of pigs and try to catch one. Every child except me had caught one of those cute pink piglets and I was determined to catch one, too, even though the other children had moved on to other entertainment after claiming their prize.

Just as I was reaching for one of the little pigs, somehow I lost my footing, tripped and fell in the pen. I was dazed and as I rolled over onto my back to try and get up, several sows were coming fast towards me. I began screaming at the top of my lungs, and the other boys and girls came running to see what the fuss was all about. When they saw what was about to happen, they too began screaming for the adults to come and save me.

I don't really remember much other than kicking both my legs as hard as I could kick, right into the snouts of at least three really large, fat and ugly sows. I do remember a big, strong, tanned and tobacco-stained hand snatching hold of my shirt and jerking me into the air. Our neighbor and friend, Jewell McCallon, had jumped into the midst of the flying fury of grunting, and angry pigs and pulled me to safety."

I can't imagine how dirty I was or how frightened Momma must have been that day. Amazingly enough, I don't remember ever having a nightmare after that or of ever being afraid of pigs."

Jewel McCallon, neighbor and friend. *Photo courtesy The Eagle, 1954 KHS Annual*

❦

Billy Smith remembered the time in the late 1960s when:

"We bought a farm in the northwest corner of Calloway County. It had some good ground and some not so good. I got the Kirksey FFA Chapter to set pine trees on the real rough land and tried to cultivate the rest of the farm. Most of the good soil was in the bottom along a creek or small stream. We grew corn on it and bought our first self-propelled combine. Billy Dale was 7 to 9 years old and thought he was big enough to help and wanted to.

I was working at Hutson's and trying to farm at night and weekends. Late one afternoon, I came home early and started to the "Klondyke" (that was what we named the farm) to shell corn. Billy Dale wanted to go along as he was home from school and said he had no homework. Off we went to shell a load or two of corn. I had borrowed a two-ton truck from Hutson and driven it home that day.

Typical 2-ton truck for hauling corn.

We got to the Klondyke and shelled our first load of corn and started back to our home place with the 300 bushels load of corn. Getting to the farm required crossing a wooden bridge over a creek. When we got to the bridge I slowed down and started across. Just as we got on to the center of bridge, it began to fall in. It was a slow but constant fall to the left and then we began to turn all the way upside down in the creek. There was a 5-gallon empty fuel can which hit me on the head as the truck turned over.

As the truck was turning over, very slowly, Billy Dale said, 'When do I jump out?' and I just said, 'Hang on!' When the truck finally came to a complete stop, it was upside down with all wheels sticking straight up. The entire 300 bushels of corn was spilled and lying in the bottom of the ditch. When the truck finally stopped turning, I told Billy Dale to go out the window and up to top of the ditch, which he did. Neither he nor I was hurt, thank the Lord, and we walked to the nearest neighbor to call Shirley to come and get us. At the house I called a wrecker to come and get the truck out of the ditch."

Billy Dale added:

"Yeah, Elmo Gardner brought his wrecker and he got it turned over and pulled it out. We couldn't believe that truck had no damage other than a mirror that was out of whack. We put water in the radiator and about a quart of oil and drove it home."

❦❧

While not necessarily a harrowing tale, one story we must tell is about our grandmother, Geneva Smith, who was well known for speed, as her grandchildren can attest. Billy remembered well one of the funnier moments where her lead foot got her into trouble:

"When Mother retired and lived south of Kirksey, being in her 70s, she and her cousin, Nitarie McCallon, and two other ladies decided to go down to Greenfield, Tenn., to a flea market or an outlet store. She had to drive her car because that was the way she was. This trip was not disclosed to any one in the family until a few years later when Bobbie and her cousin, Randy McCallon, and his wife, Janetta, were living in Shelbyville, Ky. The three of them were visiting after church one Sunday and Randy told Bobbie that his Grandmother Nitaree had told him about a trip she and Geneva had taken with two other women earlier in the summer. He reported that Granny had gotten a speeding ticket in Tennessee and had to pay a fine. This was the only way we found out about

Geneva and Reva Brewer with their cousin Nitarie (Brewer) McCallon.

the experience. We asked her about it not long afterward and she said it was true, but would not talk about it any further. Of course the grandkids and great-grandkids thought it was a hoot!"

🦋🦋

Billy Smith told another Hutson's story:

"George James was the pilot of the helicopter and we had lots of hours in it. Once we were in eastern Kentucky and weather closed in on us and we were following railroad tracks and almost flew

George James, pilot for Hutson Chemical Company, *photo courtesy Hutson marketing brochure.*

into a mountain. George said later that the map he was following did not show the tunnel that the rails went into.

Another time Shirley and I were in Central Missouri at a meeting and George came to pick us up. As we lifted up the engine had a flame-out and we came straight back down several feet for a real hard landing. George got out, told us to go back into hanger and he got out his toolbox and he and another airport official proceeded in repairing the craft. After about an hour he called for us to come and board. Shirley had a hard time believing George could fix the jet ranger helicopter, but he had, and we had a good flight home."

❦

While reminiscing about his years at Hutson's, Billy recalled another time where his duties called for him to inspect shipments of fertilizer that he'd bought when they arrived in New Orleans:

"I was responsible for being at the port and overseeing the unloading of the material. After being in New Orleans for several days the cargo was discharged into about 15 barges and I had collected 15 clear plastic bags of 46% urea. I proceeded to place them in the plane that Woody had flown us down in. I stacked the bags right next to the door on the inside of the plane. Woody cranked up and we took off and when we cleared the air strip the twin engine plane lost one of its engines. Woody declared an emergency and we circled the airport, finally getting clearance to land. As it was an emergency, when we landed, there were fire trucks following us down the runway.

When I opened the door of the plane two officers ran up the stairs as I was getting out. I went into the terminal and left Woody in the plane with the two officers. I found out shortly afterwards that the officers were extremely interested in the contents of the plastic bags. Woody had told them that it was urea but they thought it looked like dope. He had a lot of explaining to do and then they came looking for me to confirm his story. I finally got to leave New Orleans as we got a plane the next day to take us home. Unfortunately, Woody didn't get to come home for several days afterwards."

Billy Smith told this story from 1961:

"We bought a six-acre tract of land that hooked up our 40-acre farm that I'd bought when I was in high school out to the Kirksey Highway. We cleaned it off and bulldozed a spot to build us a new house. Just as we got the black paper on the roof, that was the day of the Kirksey tornado and it took the roof completely off. In addition to that damage the storm also damaged the house that we were living in at the time, raised the window and door facings away from the walls. It was so bad I could stick my hand behind every door and window facing. That night I took a hammer and re-nailed all of the facing in the house.

House that Billy and Shirley lived in, called the old Cain place.

This was also the house where, as a toddler, Bobbie kicked a one-gallon can of pink paint down the basement steps. Shirley said it was easier to just go head and paint the steps pink than to try to clean up the mess. We had the only pink basement steps in the neighborhood, and from what I understand, 49 years later, the steps are still pink!"

At the new house where Billy Dale Smith lives today:

"Porter Chilcutt, Shirley's father, came out to help us move a corn crib that we had built a couple of years before we bought the six-acre lot that gave us an exit out to the Kirksey Highway. We took the hydraulic ram that was on the tractor and lifted up each corner of the crib and put poles under the building and braced

Porter and Rubye Chilcutt, parents of Shirley (Chilcutt) Smith.

them together, then hitched the tractor to it and began to move it to its new location.

Typical corn crib in Calloway County. *Photo dated 2010.*

When we got there, we positioned it in the prepared place and unhooked the tractor from the corn crib. We pulled around and placed the hydraulic jack and began to raise the building off the sled that we had pulled it in place with. Mr. Chilcutt was holding the jack in place and it slipped and caught his thumb and finger between the hydraulic jack and the crib. After working several minutes, we finally got his hand free and carried him to the Murray Hospital emergency room. They gave him some pain medicine and tried to repair his thumb and finger. It got well, but it was never like new, and it gave him a lot of pain in his later years. I tried to be more careful after this accident when I was working with machinery and people.

After we got the house built and moved into it, Shirley was not working and was staying home with the kids and was being a wonderful mother. I was working full time at Hutson's and trying to farm at night. I was growing tobacco and trying to hire help when I could. Tobacco cutting time had come and I had eight to 12 hired hands helping cut tobacco. I would take vacation days off to work on the farm and try to get tobacco housed in less than two weeks. Some time in the late 1960s, we were cutting tobacco and Shirley

Shirley in a tobacco field 1957.

was fixing and serving lunch to all the help. We would fix a table out of a wagon to serve lunch in the back yard.

One afternoon, it was very hot and we went back to the field to continue harvesting tobacco. I became way too hot and fell out in the fence row. I would not go to the house as I stayed and tried to oversee the workers. Finally, about 3:30 p.m., Shirley brought some drinks and snacks to the field for the workers and she made me go back to the house with her. I finally got a shower and she took me to the emergency room at the Murray-Calloway County Hospital. I had become too hot and my electrolytes were nearly completely gone. They kept me in the hospital until 11 p.m. and then told me to stay home for a few days. On the way home I told Shirley that I was hungry and we stopped at a restaurant and I had a big steak. Boy, did I ever feel better. I did go to work the next day and that weekend we got the tobacco in the barns.

I had learned another lesson the hard way. I was working five days a week in an air-conditioned office, riding to and from work in an air-conditioned car and sleeping in an air-conditioned bedroom. I had become soft and unfit to work in 90- to 100-degree heat. I made a promise to Shirley and the good Lord that night at the hospital that if he would get me out and in good health, that I would stop growing tobacco as long as I was working in an air-conditioned office. I kept that promise and in just a few short years Billy Dale took over the farm and some time in the late 1980s he bought out the partnership and took over the entire farming operation."

᷍᷍

Billy Dale told about the time he was working on a combine header that had three trap doors:

"There were two safety pins on each hatch. There is always corn fodder that's accumulated inside. I'd hooked the combine to

Combining corn on Smith Farms.

the header to get it out of the barn and I was sitting cross-legged under the header. I pulled the pins and the door automatically dropped open along with all the trash inside and much to my surprise, a six-foot long chicken snake. I don't know who it scared first, the snake or me, he went one way and I went the other. I never did find that snake, even though I came back looking for it so I could kill it.

Speaking of snakes, one other time at our pond, we had a paddleboat that we'd used to fish with throughout the summer. In the early fall the boat had some water in it, so I went to flip it over and drain it. I thought to myself as I walked over to it that I needed to be sure there wasn't a snake anywhere around. Of course as I got to the boat, I didn't remember to look and as I reached out, lifting it up, I realized I was standing in a nest of snakes. Well, I started dancin' around, wound up killing at least three with my boots. I felt real stupid because I'd thought of it before I began, then forgot to look before I did it."

❧❧

Josh Smith remembered an event that terrified him, and he wasn't even the person in trouble:

"We were running in tobacco at a farm down below Kirksey when I was in high school and old enough to hand off the tobacco into the barn. I was also old enough to know right from wrong, particularly

when lives could be at stake. We're working along and all of a sudden, the Mexicans became very excited, almost panic stricken. Dad and I couldn't make out what they were saying but we knew that something wasn't right.

Typical tobacco barn in Calloway County.

One of the Mexican workers was up in the top of the barn and he was standing real still with his eyes as big as saucers. When we looked next to him, there was a family of raccoons in the corner and they were peeking out through a hole, with bared teeth. The Mexican was within just a few feet of them and they were mad that their den was being invaded. At the time, I didn't know it, but Dad had a gun in his truck. Before I had even realized what was happening, Dad had walked to his truck, taken out his pistol, and before I could really see what was going on, there were three POP, POP, POPs. As you heard each one of the pops you heard three resounding thuds, as each of the three raccoons fell dead to the floor. I remarked to Dad after the fact, 'My gosh, Dad, if you'd missed, you could have hit the Mexican,' and in his driest tone of voice, he responded, 'That's why you don't miss.'"

※※

Josh Smith recalled:

"It was a typical hot summer day about 1996 when Dad was building his first big tobacco barn, the one closest to the main shed. He had carpenters there, building each room one at a time. They'd put each room together on the ground, then lift it by a crane to stand it up. As each room

Under construction at Smith Farms.

got built, they'd attach it to the next. I was a young teenager and had been pestering the builders all day about letting me ride that crane. The very last time that the crane went up with the last room, they told me to jump on. It had a big hook and I sat with my feet wrapped around the ball and held on to a cable. They sent the room to the top of the barn where they secured it to the other sections. Then, while I was sitting there, they decided it was time for a break.

Here I am in the top of this barn, 75-80 feet in the air. The only things keeping me from falling to the ground were my sweaty palms and my feet hugging that ball, thinking that if I move at all, I'm going to fall and really hurt myself.

The carpenters taking their break, hootin' and hollerin' the entire time I was swinging up there. You do have a good view from that height, but our insurance company probably wouldn't want to know about this level of safety on our building site. They eventually brought me down, just took their good sweet time about it, giving me a hard way to go the entire time."

✺❧

Billy Dale Smith recalled:

"When I was running anhydrous in the bottoms, I had a tractor with a full set of weights on the front end. I had to come up out of the bottom field, on up a hill, and as I did, the front end reared up. I eased up on the fuel to bring it back down but when I did, I smothered the motor out and then began rolling backward. I knew I couldn't back down the hill, and of course, the wagon turned over. The tractor and the anhydrous applicator wound up on top of the wagon.

While this was happening, I thought about bailing off but was scared that I might get run over, so I just stayed on, taking my chances with it blowing up. Fortunately it didn't blow. The second time I tried it, it did the same thing again, but people who had come to help us threw some scotches under the tractor wheels to stop me, and they were able to do so. We ended up having to unhook the wagon and pull it up the hill in a four-

wheel drive truck. We had to get a wrecker to get the tractor off the wagon, then pick the wagon up and bolt the running gear back on it to move it."

❦

Josh Smith remembered:

"We were at the main barn, parking the tractor, facing south. I was about 2 or 3 years old, and I was hanging on to the door hinge with the door open. The door opened out from the tractor, and about waist high there was a hinge to keep it from going too far. Dad had gotten out to see about something and when he jumped back into the tractor he did not see my hand and slammed the door with my hands still inside holding the hinge. It broke my finger, and we had to go to the doctor for a splint. If that weren't enough, right after I got that cast off my finger, I went to Nana's Showcase and, as we were leaving, Nana shut the door of her Lincoln Continental and caught my hand in it."

❦

Billy Dale added one more harrowing moment when Josh was only 2 or 3 years old:

"He and I were in a pickup truck at Coldwater and we'd had some bulldozing done, making waterways on the farm. I was driving through grass and weeds as tall as the hood of the truck. There was a ditch out through the field and I couldn't see that it was washed out. I was only driving a few miles per hour so I didn't think anything about Josh standing in the seat next to me so he could see out.

All of a sudden the truck steered into the ditch, and Josh flew into the windshield, busting it into thousands of cracks. He hit so hard that it left his hair in some of the cracks. Of course I was scared to death that he was hurt bad. I was so worried that the truck might be stuck and that I might not get the truck out of the ditch. I threw the truck into four-wheel drive and got us out of there faster than I thought I could. I kept asking him to nod if he was okay. He kept telling me yes. He was hurt, but as it turned out he was just shaken up and had a big goose egg on his head."

CHAPTER VIII

Lighter Moments

Memorable Holidays, Special Events and Other Tales

*W*hile farm work was hard, some tasks would take on more of a fun atmosphere around harvest time. One such activity was hog-killing time—a day-long event where neighbors would help handle the animals, and there were roles for men, women and children.

Billy Smith reminisced:

"For a boy that was raised in town and spent a lot of time at his grandparents in the summer time and weekend, hog killing was something I looked forward to all year. I knew that when Thanksgiving came around that the fun time on the farm was at hand. To the people reading this that have never witnessed a hog killing, you have missed one of the most enjoyable times of the year on the farm. There would be four or five neighbor

families including men, women and children, getting together at each other's homes on different days through November and December.

Typical day of hog-killing, a tradition during harvest season. *Photo courtesy Kentucky Historical Society.*

On the appointed day, when the weather was cold enough (they wanted a clear day with the temperature below freezing in the early morning hours, warming up into the 50s during the day), the men would usually arrive early in the morning after doing their chores, about 8:30 or 9 a.m. The women would come later in the morning and help with lunch.

The men would bring the largest fat hog into a small pen and the sharpshooter of the group would take a .22 rifle and try to place a bullet between the eyes of the hog. When the hog was shot and fell, they would rush in and slit his throat to let the blood drain out of the carcass. They then placed the hog in a vat filled with water over a fire. The water had to be hot, a slow rolling boil, and they called this process scalding. After scalding, they would then roll the hog onto a scaffold and proceed to scrape off the hair. At this time, they cut a slit in the hind feet and put a 2-foot stick trimmed on both ends between the tendons and leg bone and hoisted the pig up to a large limb in a tree or to a handmade stand. Usually the first thing they did was to cut off the head, open up the hog, and take out the entrails. The meat was then cut into hams, shoulders, backbone, ribs, sides or bacon, keeping the liver and heart. The pieces were trimmed and the lean and some of the fat were put into a sausage container. The remaining fat was cut into small pieces and put into an iron kettle to make lard.

By this time, the women had made lunch and everyone was ready to eat. At that time, they had hand grinders to grind the sausage and this was a very hard job as it took a lot of

Some of the best cooks in west Kentucky, the Smith ladies in the 1960s. From left to right: Gracie (Wrather) Smith (seated), Geneva (Brewer) Smith, Bobbie (Smith) Bryant, Bettie (Smith) Stoll, Delle Smith, Shirley (Chilcutt) Smith, (standing), Haleene Smith, Ada Wrather (wife of Gratis with white ruffled blouse), and Lois (Robinson) Brewer, far right.

muscle power to turn the grinder. When the sausage was ground it was seasoned with sage, salt and pepper to the owner's taste, then put into homemade cotton sacks, about three inches in diameter and 18 inches long. The sacks were taken to a smokehouse and hung up to cure. The fat, after being cut up into small pieces, was placed in the kettles with fires under them. One man would take a lard paddle and stir the fat pieces to keep them from burning. As they got the kettle hot, the grease cooked out of the fat and the fat turned into cracklings. When all the grease had cooked out of the fat, the cracklings were squeezed with a squeezer, (two four-inch planks put together at one end with a door hinge and used as a squeeze). The cracklings were picked up with a large dipper and put in a linen cloth. The cloth was then squeezed, to get the grease out. The remaining grease was then poured into a lard can and left to set so that it becomes lard as it cooled.

Typical shed in Calloway County.

Then, they would hang the liver and heart of the pig in the smokehouse and would eat on it until it spoiled. They would take the head and remove the brains to cook with eggs for breakfast for the next several days. They used the rest of the head to make souse meat. The feet would be pickled and were to be eaten as delicacies later. Cracklings were used to flavor cornbread for several months and usually there were some sweetbreads in them as well, which were very good.

After the lard had been drained and everything halfway cleaned up, someone would come up with three or four ears of popcorn, shell them and put the popcorn in the iron kettle with some of the settlings left over *from the lard making and pop the corn for everyone before they went home. I wonder how many kids today know where popcorn comes from other than out of the microwave."*

Billy Dale remembered one hog killing when he was very young at Papa Brewer's at Penny:

"There were three or four hogs, there was a yard full of people and everyone had their own job to do. We always ate our own home-cured meat, and back then I always thought it was kind of nasty, so I wanted city-bought bacon—not as big, thick and salty as what we made fresh. Now, when I think back to that fresh hog jowl, sausage and bacon, my mouth just waters."

❦

Sausage Breakfast Casserole

1 lb. sausage, cooked and drained

8 oz. mozzarella cheese

4 eggs, beaten

¾ cup milk

2 tbsp. chopped green peppers

½ tsp. salt/pepper

½ tsp. oregano

Biscuits or rolls, baked as directed

Grease baking dish and put rolls or biscuits in the bottom. Sprinkle cooked sausage on the bread, then the cheese. Combine all other ingredients, beat well and pour over the other items. Bake at 425 degrees for 20-25 minutes. Yields 6 servings.

❦

In *Kentucky: Land of Contrast*, Dr. Thomas Clark reminds us: "Since the days that the early settlers dragged a deer into a pioneer fort, Kentuckians have liked food, in great quantities. Whether it be a meal at a private dining table or an outdoor dinner, they liked to be surrounded by food in plenty. A rural outdoor church dinner in 1905 might not have competed handily with fancy city food in daintiness or appearance, or in the order of the service, but it was well ahead in flavor. Kentucky cooks at the turn of the century did not know the meaning of calories, let alone reasonable portions."

Kentucky Hospitality: A 200 Year Tradition points out that there were two other factors beyond ethnicity that affected foodways in Kentucky: the desire to improve one's status in life, and geography. Kentucky's natural environment is ideal for fostering a variety of foods. As the state developed and roads led from one region to another, traditional foods were cross-pollinated with those from other cultures. The results were pure Kentucky.

Billy Smith remembered Mama Brewer's dinner table very well:

Lois (Robinson) Brewer, with baby daughter Geneva, and Floy Brewer.

"It was a favorite place for a growing boy. She did not have a refrigerator and would leave the food on the table. It was always covered with a newspaper. Under that paper there were always cold baked sweet potatoes, tea cakes, and a meat dish in the center of the table filled with leftover meat. I could always find something to eat during the day by sneaking around her table and enjoying the leftovers from the last meal. Most of the time I could find a piece of country ham, maybe a sausage cake or a slice of bacon. I could scrape off the cold grease that was always in bottom of dish but it was good eating to a 4- to 8-year-old growing boy. Mama Brewer always said that she could send me with a cup to the barn when Papa was milking and I would get him to fill my cup with fresh warm milk and ruin my appetite for supper."

Tea Cakes

2½ cups flour

¼ tsp. salt

2 tsp. baking powder

1 cup sugar

½ cup butter

2 eggs, beaten

3 tbsp. milk

¼ tsp. vanilla or lemon extract

Sift together flour, salt, baking powder and sugar. Add butter and beaten eggs. Mix well. Add milk and flavoring. Turn into floured board. Roll thin, cut and place on an ungreased cookie sheet. Sprinkle with sugar. Bake at 400 degrees for 10 to 12 minutes or until lightly browned. Yield 4 dozen cookies.

Birthdays are always celebrated in the Smith family, especially for the children. Having family, neighbors and classmates over for the fun is usually part of the celebration. And any children in Calloway County who have never been 'snipe' hunting don't know what they've missed.

Josh explained:

"On my 10th birthday Dad told me that we could have 10 kids over. We had pizza and jumped on the trampoline in the back yard, and played like crazy. Later that night, Dad asked if any of us boys had ever been snipe hunting.

Billy Smith's third birthday.

When going Snipe hunting, this is the critter for which one should be searching. *Photo courtesy U.S. Fish and Wildlife Service website.*

Well, Mom had just bought our family an Encyclopedia Britannica so we looked up snipes and there was a picture of one in the book. So Dad told us that we'd go snipe hunting. He instructed us on the proper way to hunt for snipe, telling us that we'd have to be oh so quiet and lay in wait until they came up. He lined us up around a small pond in one of the fields and spread us apart from each other. He told us that he'd go over to the other section of the farm and try to spook them enough to scare them over to us so we could catch them.

We were all so quiet, whispering back and forth as to whether anyone could see any snipes anywhere. We stayed out there for well over an hour and finally gave up. We got together and trudged back to the house, a bit hapless that we hadn't seen, let alone caught a snipe. When we got back to the house, there sat Dad, watching TV, eating popcorn, asking us, 'Well, did you ever find them?' Needless to say we were undone about the whole thing."

Another Josh birthday memory:

"On my 13th birthday I had a classmate who was also a neighbor, and she and I shared the same birthday. Our parents made joint invitations and we had about 30 to 40 kids for a birthday party out at the barn. We played music and danced, had a great time. Dad had told me to explain to them once they got there that as we were on the farm and around the farm equipment, anything they touched would probably get them dirty. One girl spoke up and said: 'Yeah, and if you don't believe, him, look at my pants.'

As it got dark we all jumped into the back of the gooseneck trailer for a hayride. We had to climb up about 10 feet high to get in the trailer, so we had to use a ladder. We went the back roads and rode around a while and then we stopped at Asbury graveyard. We all got out and walked around looking at grave stones, trying not to act as though we were scared. All of a sudden, somebody dressed in black from the back of the cemetery stood up and yelled out in a deep, spooky voice, 'All you kids get out of here!' We did not need the ladder to get everybody back into the truck—they were diving in, screaming their heads off! As we started back, it began to rain and everyone got absolutely soaked before we got back to the farm. It was one of the best birthdays I remember, and everybody had a great time, in spite of the dirt and the rain."

Typical hayride on flat bed wagon at Smith Farms, this one a Twilight Farm Tour. Hayrides held after dark are inside a wagon or truck with sideboards for further safety.

🦋

According to *Kentucky: Land of Contrast*: "Near the end of the nineteenth century when the Grand Army of the Republic held its convention in Louisville, the city offered every form of entertainment which its promoters believed would gladden old soldiers' hearts. Proclaiming in 1890s style, and for local public consumption, that Louisville was home of churches, schools, theatres and art museums, the copywriters created a fine image for the place. More imaginative sons, however took advantage of the heartbeat of the veterans away from home and the inhibitions of churches, theaters and schools, and offered them culture of another sort. The kind of art that many an old veteran wanted to learn about was displayed along Green Street and its adjoining alleys. The 'bluebook' issued for this occasion was a highly informative guide to visitors and comrades-in-arms. The book promised, however to shatter domestic tranquility back home for any 'Billy Yank' who forgot to toss it out of his coat pocket on his departure from Louisville."

Although no bluebook was published, word got out about this type of entertainment and occasionally the citizens of Calloway County left the farm for other forms of enjoyment. Billy Smith told about one memory from his senior year when Harvey Ellis and Leroy Eldridge, ag teachers at Kirksey and Murray Training School, took a car load from each school to the National FFA convention in Kansas City, Missouri:

FFA Kirksey Chapter, *photo courtesy 1955 Kirksey High School annual, featuring Billy Smith as president in the center at the table.*

"This was a great learning experience. There were several thousand Ag boys with their blue FFA jackets on. Quite a sight to see that many boys with all the same jackets. Kansas City was a big city for us and there were lots of things to do and see. One thing that caught our attention was the burlesque shows.

Harvey and Leroy told us not to go to the shows. Well, after about the second night, they took us back to the hotel, and we all went to our rooms. We had made up during the day that we would go to the burlesque show that night. We waited about a half hour and then we slipped out of our rooms and went downstairs and slipped out of the hotel. We walked the two or three blocks and bought our tickets and went inside. It was dark and we finally found some seats down in the middle of the room. The program was under way and we were enjoying the show.

Intermission came and they turned on the lights and down in front of us about six or eight rows sat Mr. Ellis and Mr. Eldridge. You talk about boys sinking down in their seats. We did, and stayed real quiet. When the lights went out we were quite relieved. We stayed and watched most of the show, but we left early so the teachers would not see us. On the way home, Harvey asked if we enjoyed the burlesque show. We were afraid to say anything and then he told us they had slipped in to be sure that we did not get into more trouble than we could get out of. We have laughed about this several times since. Boys will be boys, and the older men know it and will try to protect them."

❧❧

Shirley (Chilcutt) Smith and daughter Bobbie clowning around in the 1970s in preparation for Halloween.

Traditional holidays remain very much a part of the Smith family culture. Halloween was always celebrated, and the Kirksey community is notorious for having a fire set each year. This is a common occurrence in small communities across the county. The most common were fires set in the middle of a highway, burning such things as tires, leaves, and straw.

Recollections of Calloway County recounts that the concept of a fire goes back to the idea of burning witches at the stake to purify the area of evil spirits. Most young people who now set fires do not even think of evil spirits; a fire in the middle of the road is just something different to do. Bettie Smith Stoll recalled:

"Every Halloween some 'people' always kept a bonfire going at the crossroads in Kirksey and one Halloween some 'people' put Papa Brewer's wagon in the Kirksey High School Gymnasium, up on the stage."

Billy Smith confessed to being one of those people:

"Yes, Kirksey always got a new outhouse after Halloween as we boys

Billy Smith with his own Halloween costume.

would drag it out to the center of the crossroad and put several old tires around it and sprinkle some oil on them and set them on fire. This went on for several years. Then one year we had a new sheriff and he caught several of us and told us that if we did it the next year that there would be big trouble in Kirksey. Apparently the fire from the past year had burned a big hole in the blacktop and the State Highway Department was going to punish the people the next time that it occurred.

This stopped the burning of the outhouses and tires, but the boys soon discovered that bales of wheat straw and a small load of corncobs made a really big and hot fire as good as or better than the outhouse. Cellular telephones finally brought an end to the fires in Kirksey on Halloween."

Other tricks that have been pulled in the county include egging—throwing eggs at unsuspecting people or targets. Another trick is that of covering the yard of a neighbor—friend or foe—with toilet paper, which creates a particularly nasty mess after a rain. Other farm folk found it more fun to play on their friend's nerves, as Billy Dale Smith shared:

"One Halloween when trick or treaters came to the house, they had on white long johns with white sacks over their heads. They came in, sat down and just sat there with us, never said a word. After a while, they got up and left. It was really eerie and we never did know who they were."

Many children simply have fun with the treating side of Halloween, dressing up and attending a special fall festival or going door to door, seeking candy at neighbors' homes. The Smith family has enjoyed Halloween through the years with parties and hayrides. Scavenger hunts, apple bobbing, pumpkin throwing, and other games are a requirement. Every hayride

Harvest time at Smith Farms, always a special time of celebration.

winds up at some point during the evening at Asbury graveyard, a particularly scary place at night.

Billy Smith confessed:

"The meanest trick that I was involved in was one year when tobacco cutting was very late and Mr. Washer had his tobacco scaffolds on his wagon, sitting by his big pond. The pond had been cleaned out the year before and was a depth of some seven or eight feet. As we drove by that Halloween night, someone in the back seat said how much fun it would be to push that wagon into the pond. We tried and we were not big enough to do it, but when we went to town, we found some help and it only took nine of us boys to complete the job. Mr. Washer looked for his wagon and scaffolds all winter. During the summer drought when the water in the pond went down a few feet, Mr. Washer found his wagon and tobacco scaffolds."

⁓⁓

Christmas in the early days of Kentucky was simple but joyous. Many a farm child found great pleasure in decorating a cedar tree cut from the farm, using popcorn strung on thread and making homemade ornaments. Billy Smith recalled:

"My first remembrance of Christmas was when I was 4 or 5 years old. We would always spend Christmas Eve with Papa and Mama Brewer, along with my cousins, Jo Nell and Sharon Story, and their parents, Harvey and Reva Brewer Story, mother's sister and her husband. This was during World War II, and Harvey worked at the munitions plant north of Mayfield and Mother and Dad ran the little grocery store. This

is where Santa Claus came to visit Bettie and myself, as well as Jo Nell and Sharon.

Billy Smith with his prized bicycle at their home in Mayfield.

The Christmas that stands out the most was the year I got my bicycle. I was old enough to think there was not a real Santa Claus, and I know I had searched Papa's house real good and could not find Santa Claus anywhere. I had watched Dad load the car and I did not think I was going to get my long sought-after present. The night was fairly warm, and we had an extremely bad fog.

Uncle Harvey was working the late shift and had to drive to Papa's house around midnight, after he got off from work. I stayed up until they made me go to bed, and then I tried to stay awake after I went to bed because I wanted to see Santa Claus. After I made a couple of attempts to spy on Santa Claus, I finally fell asleep after being told to go back to bed. Christmas morning came and when I woke up, to my great surprise and joy, there were two bicycles around the tree, one for Jo Nell and one for me. The weather was bad and the ground was muddy and I had to wait until after lunch when we went back to Papa and Mama Smith's for Christmas dinner before I could ride my new bicycle on the sidewalk in front of the grocery store that they ran.

Another thing that really stands out about my Christmases is what we got in our stockings. The only time we ever had all the fresh fruit and nuts that we wanted was at Christmas. We would hang our socks over the back of a chair, close to the Christmas tree. There would always be pecans, walnuts, hazel nuts and Brazil nuts in the socks along with an orange, apple, bananas, tangerine and chewing gum. Fresh fruit was

When an attic fire destroyed Billy and Shirley's collection of Christmas decorations in 1981, Bobbie Smith created personalized Christmas stockings for each family member. The collection has grown through the years as new members of the family have been added. *Photo taken in 1997.*

not available all year round like it is now, and this was always a treat that I looked forward to. I would gorge myself and be too full to eat at lunch and dinner time. To this day I still enjoy fresh fruit and we try to keep fresh apples, bananas, melons and nuts to munch on every day during the year.

Christmas is still a fun time of the year, and I especially enjoyed playing Santa when our kids, Billy Dale and Bobbie Ann, were small. I remember when Billy Dale was about 3 years old, I bought him a Texaco Service Station. I stayed up most of the night putting it together. It had little cars, a grease rack that raised and lowered, miniature oil cans, gas pumps and several other items, just like his Papaw Porter's service station. Billy Dale got up and went to the service station and began to play with it, and it wasn't five minutes before it came all apart. The thing that he liked most was a fairly large Texaco gas trailer truck made of metal that he could straddle and ride around on the clean polished floor that Mother was so proud of.

I think one of the best Christmases that Bobbie had was when she discovered a Barbie doll under the tree. She played with it all day and I think she still cherishes it to this day. Santa never failed in being

Bobbie Smith showing off her Barbie doll in photo featured in the Farm Bureau News in 1965.

good to me and I hope my children and grandchildren never have to be disappointed at Christmas."

Bobbie Smith Bryant recalled Christmas at her great-grandparents home:

"When we were really small we would go to our Mama and Papa Brewer's and our cousins would be there. They always had a nice tree with colored lights."

Billy Dale joined in the memory:

"Remember, they'd always do sparklers and fireworks for Christmas. One year they had a chaser that went up Aunt Bettie's skirt and scared the whole family as it burned her leg very badly before she could get rid of it. Santa Claus would always come but they'd turn out the lights and you couldn't see him very well."

ᗧᖇ

Easter, Thanksgiving and Christmas are celebrated in a traditional style by the Smiths. Each holiday brings out the best in the family cooks, preparing traditional and delectable dishes. Roasted turkey, sliced ham, mashed sweet potatoes, green beans, baked apples, yeast rolls and cranberry salad are holiday delights. Deviled eggs, sweet pickles and radishes are garnishes that grace every holiday meal. If those tasty treats weren't enough, we top all this off with sweet tea or strong coffee while choosing from desserts of coconut cake, peach or blackberry cobbler, meal or pecan pie.

Typical food fest at the Smith's during the holidays.

COCONUT THREE-LAYER CAKE   *by Geneva Smith*

8 tbsp. butter, room temperature (1 stick)

2 cups sugar

1 cup canola oil

2 egg yolks

2 cups flour, all-purpose

1 tsp. baking soda

1 cup buttermilk

1 tsp. vanilla extract

1½ cups coconut, flaked, sweetened

1 cup pecan pieces (optional)

5 egg whites, stiffly beaten

Preheat oven to 350° F

Cream butter, add sugar and beat until smooth. Add egg yolks and canola oil to mixture.

In another bowl, combine flour and baking soda. Alternately add flour, baking soda and buttermilk to batter. Stir in vanilla, coconut, and nuts. Fold in egg whites. Pour batter into three greased and floured cake pans.

Bake the cake at 350 degrees for 25 to 30 minutes or until a wooden toothpick comes out clean.

Cool cake, add cream cheese icing between cake layers, then sides, and top last. Keep refrigerated.

CREAM CHEESE ICING

8 oz. cream cheese, softened

4 tbsp. butter, softened (not melted)

1 tsp. vanilla extract

1 lb. confectioners' sugar

3 pkg. coconut, grated, frozen (6 oz bag)

Mix all ingredients together with electric mixer.

The Smith family toasting the New Year. From left to right back row: Josh Smith, Geneva (Brewer) Smith, Hal Smith, Porter Chilcutt, and Evelyn (Ahart Wilson) Chilcutt (Porter's second wife). Front row left to right: Billy Dale Smith, Sheila (Kirk) Smith, Shirley (Chilcutt) Smith, Billy Smith and partially shown is the white fur ball known as Jessie, Bobbie Smith's dog. *Bobbie was taking the picture at Smith Farms in late 1980s.*

Ringing in the New Year has always been a reason to celebrate. As at Christmas, revelers are prepared for New Year's Eve with Roman candles, sparklers, cherry bombs and bottle rockets.

Family traditions also hold true in terms of good food for New Year's Day. Black-eyed peas and some form of greens will always be served on the first day of the year. The peas represent coin money while the greens represent cash. The menu also typically involves hog-jowl, mashed potatoes and cornbread. The greens may be cabbage, turnip greens, kale, or mustard greens that are usually boiled with a ham hock for seasoning along with a large onion, peeled and chopped. A teaspoon of sugar and one of dry mustard, with a splash of apple cider vinegar, makes for some tasty greens—even for those who don't think they like greens.

Bobbie's Favorite Sweet Cornbread

1¼ cups all purpose flour
¾ cups corn meal
¼ cup sugar
2 tsp. baking powder
½ tsp. salt
1 cup milk
¼ cup vegetable oil
2 eggs, beaten

Heat oven to 400 degrees. Grease an 8- or 9-inch iron skillet. Combine dry ingredients. Stir in milk, oil and egg, mixing just until dry ingredients are moistened. Pour batter into prepared pan. Bake 20 to 25 minutes or until light golden brown and wooden pick inserted in center comes out clean. Serve warm. About 8 servings.

Another tradition passed along from Shirley Smith is that of placing a shiny new penny on the front door stoop on New Year's Eve. First thing on New Year's Day, pick up the penny and bring it in the house for good luck all year long.

Farm Animals, Critters and Pets

Farm animals have been an important part of the Smith family for many years, providing fodder for some of our best family stories.

Billy Smith shared this story:

"Papa Brewer had goats, and he had one special billy goat. The goat always had a chain around his neck that hung down and drug between his feet. I was always challenged by that goat and wanted to catch him as he was forever tempting me. One day I slipped up behind him and got both hands on that chain and did I ever have a wild ride! He drug me around the house and out into the woods where there was a blackberry patch. He ran into the briars dragging me right along, stopping right in the middle of the patch.

There I lay scratched, bleeding, and scared to

Josh Smith shown with twin goats, following in the footsteps of his dad and Aunt Bobbie.

death, but I would not turn loose of the chain and the chain was caught around a small bush and the goat could not get away. Papa and Mama heard the commotion of me crying and that goat bellowing and came running to see what I had gotten into. Papa had to put on his work gloves and use an ax to get to the billy goat and me out of the brambles. They cleaned me up, patched my scars and got rid of that old goat the very next week."

Mamma Brewer's Blackberry Cobbler

2 tbsp. butter or margarine

½ cup sweet milk

2/3 cup flour

pinch of salt

½ cup sugar

1 quart blackberries

1 cup sugar

Mix butter, milk, flour, salt and ½ cup sugar; put in baking dish. Coat blackberries (or your choice of fruit) with 1 cup sugar and pour over batter. Bake at 350 degrees for 20-30 minutes until bubbly.

Goats have been on Smith family farms for several generations. Billy Smith recalled when Bobbie and Billy Dale were young, Shirley would have them take naps in the afternoons:

"At that time we had an old goat, and naturally she was named Nanny. Nanny goat would lie on the front porch under the window of the kids' bedrooms and take a nap when they did, after lunch. One day, Nanny decided to have some babies and from what Shirley said about the day, both kids performed as midwife for Nanny and her newborn twins."

Billy Smith also recalled one Thanksgiving Day around 1950 or 1951 when animals proved to be more helpful than motorized vehicles:

"Mayfield always played Paducah Tilghman in football on Thanksgiving Day. On this particular day the game was to be played in Paducah, and we could not attend as Papa Brewer had sold his farm and bought another farm behind were we live today. We call it the Cain place.

Thanksgiving Day was his moving day and I wanted to be part of it. He had a spotted pony and I got to ride the horse all the way from the old farm to the next one, about 5 miles. That morning, it was cool and clear, but at about 10 a.m. it started to cloud up and turned real cold. It started to snow sometime in early afternoon. I was riding the horse and trying to help with all the other animals that the men were moving. Finally, just after noon, Papa told me to ride on to the new house, which I did. After about another hour I thought I would freeze. I got off the small horse and walked, leading her to the new barns.

Late that afternoon or early evening, Mother and Dad came up from Mayfield after closing the store and said it was beginning to snow. The next morning there was a big snow and that Sunday afternoon as we tried to go home by car, we got in a snow drift in middle of road and the car would go no further. Dad had to walk back to Papa's new home and get him and a team of mules to come and pull the car all the way out to the Kirksey highway."

❧❧

Billy Dale Smith recalled:

"Our Momma has always been scared of snakes, so me and Bobbie are naturally scared of them, too. One time on the north side of the chicken house, there was a chicken snake that ate a bullfrog. I laugh every time I think about it, you could see

Shirley in the bean field, scaring away the snakes!

that frog jumping up and down in the snake's belly, and Momma was chasing the snake around with the hoe to chop its head off.

Because of my fear, I'm always aware of snakes that are likely going to be in the tobacco barns, but you never know where they'll be. I'm really scared of copperheads and we've found two of them before. When we're going in to fill the barn with tobacco, we're always looking out for them.

One time when I was at our Granddaddy Hal's barn with him, he spotted a chicken snake and he asked me for a stick. When I found out what he wanted to do with it, before I gave it to him, I told him he'd better not flip that snake on me or we'd have a problem. Fortunately, when he flipped it, it fell away from me."

Josh Smith offered an early snake memory from when he was about 5 years old:

"Dad had a plant bed, and this was back before the newer methods of setting tobacco when you had to hand-pick the plants that had been sewn in the plant beds. When the plants were a certain height, you'd get on your hands and knees and pull them out, filling a basket, then you'd go to the setter and plant 'til you ran out of what you had in your basket.

This particular day, the plant bed was covered with white canvas, and it was warm enough that I was barefooted. I was playing and running across the road next to the house and there was a broken phone pole that was down in the tall grass. There were no wires, just a downed pole. As I got around that pole and in the tall grass, something hissed and I didn't know what it was. I hollered for Dad that something was hissing at me. He came over to see what I'd found and killed a black racer with the broken pole.

He pulled the snake out from under the pole and laid it out for me to look at and used it to teach me about snakes in general, trying to reassure me that it would not kill me if it were to bite me. As we got finished with the lesson, we started back toward the setter. As I was only 5 years of age, I thought we needed to bury it, just as you would any animal. I asked Dad about that, but he told me that the birds would take care of it, so I went on back with him and started playing again."

For as long as the Smith family can remember, pets have been part of the farm and family. Each of us has special favorites. Billy Smith remembered his favorite dogs:

"My first dog was a white Spitz, and I called him Snowball. I cannot remember where we got him or who might have given him to me, but I well remember playing with that dog when I was very young. I also remember when I started to school he wanted to follow me and had to be tied up until I came home in the afternoons. He would ride with me on my bicycle in a basket mounted on the handlebars.

I got my second dog sometime before we left Mayfield. He was a black Cocker Spaniel named Jim. The first thing we had to do was bob tail him. I remember Dad took the pup and I helped hold him while Dad took the meat

Billy Smith with his beloved dog, Snowball.

cleaver and chopped off his tail. Mother took some bandages and taped him up. Jim lived to be 14 years old. We have pictures of Billy Dale and

Bobbie playing with him when they were young. They were the ones who finally admitted to putting a rubber band around his neck so he'd have a collar, and it was so tight, he finally died from it. I found him under some bushes around the house and discovered the rubber band and saw that it

Bobbie and Billy Dale with Jim.

Billy Smith with his father-in-law, Porter Quincy Chilcutt in the late 1950s.

was infected. I took him to the vet but he was too far gone and died in a day or two. We buried him at the farm where both kids started their growing up.

My third dog was a bird dog pup that Shirley's father gave to me when we first married. Porter, her dad, loved to bird hunt and taught me what little I know about bird hunting today. I named the dog Ruby, and Shirley has never forgiven me for naming the dog after her mother."

❧

Bobbie Smith Bryant remembered having a spotted Shetland pony named Patsy:

"Patsy was such a docile horse, except if you walked behind her, she would always kick. We learned early on not to go behind her. Billy Dale and I were just little ones, 5 or 6 years old, when we had her. We'd play cowboy and Indians out in the back yard and we'd make a running leap to get up on Patsy's back, just as the Indians we watched on TV would do, without using a saddle. That poor horse, she'd just stand there and let us jump up and off, all afternoon.

One thing we knew about Patsy was that she would not run, trot or

Bobbie (Smith) Bryant in her Indian Princess costume riding on Patsy, her Shetland pony in 1966.

Bobbie riding our Palomino pony named Ginger.

gallop. She had only one gait, walking. Slowly. The only time I remember her ever getting in a hurry was one winter when we'd had really cold weather and the pond had frozen over. I was riding her out to go across the pond and we heard this really loud POP. Thank goodness for both of us, she ran for the shoreline as the ice began to give way.

I also remember Papa Brewer having a beautiful Palomino horse named Ginger that was so well trained she would round up the cattle and could back up to close a fence gate so Papa wouldn't have to get off and go do it himself. For some reason Ginger came to live with us at our farm. She was a great horse to ride, but I was a bit afraid of her. It seemed like every time I'd get on for a ride, she'd get spooked somehow and take off with me barely hanging on. After getting thrown a few times, I decided horses were not for me."

☙❧

Bobbie also remembered: *"As we were growing up, Billy Dale and I each got a white rabbit one year for Easter. We were probably in the first or second grade in school at the time. We would*

Billy Dale and Bobbie loved animals and the rabbits were an Easter addition that kept on multiplying.

feed them carrots and lettuce leaves. We hadn't had them too long when Daddy started having to build cages to keep more rabbits as we seemed to have a new round of babies pretty often. I'd say about a year or two after we got them, we began to run out of room for additional cages and we began giving them away."

⚛️

Josh Smith remembered a dog from his childhood:

Billy Dale's dog named Nip.

"When I was in the fourth grade, Dad had an old dog named Nip. He'd been with us forever. I grew up with Nip, sweetest dog we've ever had, I guess you could say he was like my brother. Nip was so gentle, he would sleep with the cat; they always got along real well. When he got to be around 13 or 14 years old, he could no longer hear and was very arthritic. He was lying in the driveway one day and one of the fertilizer trucks came through. The driver thought the dog would move, but as he didn't, the truck couldn't stop in time and ran over him.

Nip did not die, but could not move. I saw what it had done to him, and knew that he was in bad shape, but I would not let Dad kill him. He was pitiful, drug himself under a bush but I couldn't bear to have him put down. When I went to school the next day, I probably went to get my temperature taken about 15 times so I could go home and be with my dog. Finally the school nurse called Mom and told her what I was doing, wanting to go home. Of course I wanted to check on Nip, so Mom finally came and got me and took me home. I went straight away to sit with Nip and hold him as he was still alive, but in bad shape.

Josh Smith and the dog he grew up with, Nip.

Dad came outside and sat with me while we hugged and loved on Nip. Mom eventually came and got me to go to my grandmother Dot's (Dorothy Kirk) house. I didn't know why we were going, just that I had to go with Mom. When I got back, I ran to find Nip, but he was not there. I was bawling, he had been like my brother, it was just too much to bear that he was gone. Dad came home and sat with me while I was crying, he hugged me and he was crying too. He showed me where he'd buried him and about every day when I got home from school, I'd go sit where he was buried.*

When I got older, dad told me that when he had to put him down (country folk have to put their own dogs down, they don't generally go to the vet), he couldn't bring himself to shoot the dog himself. He told me, 'I had to have one of the men who worked for us to do it for me, you know how I felt about that dog.'"

Hunting, Sports and Other Forms of Entertainment

Hunting, fishing, basketball, football, and tractor pulls have served as entertainment for the Smith family through the years. Hunters in west Kentucky enjoy large populations of deer, rabbit, squirrel, quail, wild turkey, dove, and waterfowl, as recorded in *Clark's Kentucky Almanac*. With more navigable waterways than any other state in the continental United States, fishing and bird hunting are readily available in Kentucky.

A History of Kentucky notes that the Tennessee Valley Authority (TVA) began in 1964 by acquiring more than 115,000 acres of privately owned land as part of the Kentucky Woodland National Wildlife Refuge. This picturesque area of natural lands between the Cumberland and Tennessee rivers was opened to the public in 1968 as a recreational area, providing a paradise for fishing in Kentucky. With crappie, bass, and catfish being most frequently sought after, most members of the Smith family enjoy fishing as a leisure sport and for good eating.

Bobbie's Baked Fish

Your choice white fish: Catfish, Trout, Talapia, Cod, Haddock, etc.

8 oz. sour cream

1 pkg. dry Ranch Dressing Mix

Salt and pepper

Durkees French Fried Onions

8 oz. mayonnaise

Mix equal parts of sour cream and mayo. Add dry Ranch Dressing Mix and salt and pepper.

Coat fish thoroughly in sour cream mixture and roll in crushed fried onions.

Bake at 350 degrees for 10-15 minutes or until done.

Traditional Fried Fish

Catfish

Salt/pepper

Egg or milk, beaten with 1 tablespoon water

Cornmeal

Fat for frying

Fish should be filleted before frying. Wash and drain the fish; sprinkle with salt/pepper. Dip the fish in the egg or milk then coat with cornmeal. Fry in ¼ inch hot fat until brown on one side, then turn and brown on the other side, 3 to 5 minutes.

Billy Dale Smith with his
prized deer.

White tail deer are one of the favorite game animals for hunters in Kentucky. Billy Dale Smith told about the first deer he ever killed:

"I was on Joe Dunn's farm and I'd been seeing tracks for a year or two on the farm and everyone was laughing at me because no one had ever seen them out there. They'd tease me that I was seeing cattle or goat tracks. So one day I went down there and sat for hours without seeing a single deer. After a long time I got fed up and went back to my truck and as soon as I got there, here came the deer. I got back out of the truck and shot one, bringing home my prize. Guess I finally was able to prove my word."

Billy Dale Smith has become known in the family and the area for his smoked venison:

"Salt the meat real well and soak in soy sauce. Sometimes I add either barbeque sauce or some sort of salad dressing like French or honey, sweet or spicy. Place the meat in a smoker and smoke until done."

Josh recalled his first gun:

"Dad has never been what you'd call a great hunter, but he always went hunting. When I was about 10, I wanted a BB gun real bad. Pap gave me $14 to buy one, but I had to pay him back and he wanted a dollar in interest. I liked the BB gun and shot with it a lot, but I couldn't hit much of anything. When I got a bit older, Pap gave me his 20-gauge

Browning, from Belgium. I didn't know much about guns at the time, but I knew this one was special."

🦅🦅

Josh Smith remembered his dad's efforts to get him to go deer hunting:

"I was just 13 and liked to sleep in of a morning. When he thought I was old enough, he wanted me to go to a hunter's safety course, so I did. It was to be held on a Thursday and Friday night. Now keep in mind, I'm a football player at the time and this particular night there was a fellow named Dick Butkus speaking at the gym of our school, to a big crowd. The hunter's safety course I was to take was to be held in the cafeteria in the same school where Butkus was to speak. Sure enough, Dad made me go to the safety course instead of Butkus' speech and I couldn't talk him out of it. Dick Butkus was less than 100 yards away from me, and I was in a hunter safety class, hearing about stuff that I already knew.

About two weeks later, Dad told me that we'd wake up early the next day and go hunting. About 3:30 a.m. he woke me up. Naturally, it was freezing outside. We went to the Kirksey store and got our ham and biscuits for breakfast and went out to the farm to hunt. About 5 a.m. we got to the tree stand and I promptly fell asleep. After I woke up, it was cold and I was apparently making too much racket. As time went by, I got even more fidgety. Sometime before daylight, we heard the deer blow, but we never saw the deer and yet we knew it was there. I suppose I'd scared it off with my fidgeting.

We went back to the house and that afternoon, Dad asked if I wanted to go back out and try again, and I did. We went somewhere else on the farm, in a low spot in the field. We settled down in there. I was much more comfortable as it wasn't cold and I wasn't as fidgety. We couldn't talk, we were just sitting there waiting on the deer to show up. All of a sudden, I see two mice that were running around just inches away from me. I wanted to jump up, but I knew I had to sit still. After about 30 minutes, Dad finally took me back home, and I've never been hunting with him again."

🦅🦅

Porter Chilcutt and his neighbor Mr. Fuller shown with their bird dogs.

Bird hunting also has been popular in the family, and several members enjoyed the sport together. Billy Smith told of one of his favorite hunts:

"Charles Chilcutt, Shirley's brother, my father-in-law, Porter, and I had many good bird hunts. I especially remember taking Billy Dale hunting with his first 20-gauge shotgun. We had Ruby, the bird dog that Porter had trained, and one of her pups that we were trying to train that day. We were in a honeysuckle fence row and Ruby pointed a covey of birds. They came up and Billy Dale killed his first bird. The rest of the covey flew off and landed, scattered down the fence row of honeysuckle. That was one of the most fun days of my life watching Billy Dale kill his first birds and the pup point his first birds."

❧❦

November marks the beginning of the annual migration of thousands of ducks and geese through Kentucky, particularly the western part of the state. Kentucky Lake and Barkley Lake are ideally suited for great waterfowl hunting. Most hunters with an interest in goose or duck hunting travel to the Ballard County Refuge, known for years as "The Goose Capital of the World."

Billy Dale Smith enjoys the sport of goose and duck hunting:

"Dad started me out when I was about 14 years old. We'd always been bird hunters, but this was a lot easier as we'd go to a blind and the birds would come to us. We started out at the refuge in Ballard County, and I ran into a buddy that hunted at Kentucky and Barkley Lakes. Being young, I didn't have a lot of concern about being in the lake at winter

Billy Dale Smith on his first goose hunting expedition with Dad.

time. There were lots of times when we'd go out and the weather would be pretty, but when we come back, it was a different story. I've seen years where ice was so thick that we'd have to run the boat and motor up and on the ice and then break the ice to get out. I've also seen water so rough that tugboats pushing barges would have to tie off at the bank because they weren't making headway in the wind. We've had boats quit in the lake and have to push them back along the shoreline. I found out real quick why we all had to have hip waders on.

There was one time when I was standing out in the middle of the lake in shallow water with a Chesapeake dog that belonged to someone else. The owner told me to scold the dog for chewing up one of the birds and I did. When the dog began growling at me, I wondered why I ever got on to him in the first place.

I'd always take extra socks with me in case I got wet. One time when I was out on an island, the ground around the island was real muddy and I got water and mud in my boots and I got my feet real wet. When I got back to the blind I was able to clean up and put on dry socks. That was one time I was really glad to have an extra pair of socks while hunting.

One year when the lake froze over, we drove over to Hickman with 12 people going to a duck blind. The bay was frozen over and our guide told us if we could get enough ice chipped away to get the boat in, we could go across to the blind. We had to ride the boat up on the ice to get out, and when we got to the blind, we were ready to get out of the boat while the guide went back and got the rest of the hunters. However, they were afraid it might refreeze before he got back with the others, so they had us to ride back across with him to get the other hunters. They had a good hunting day but when I think back on it, we were real stupid to risk that as we did."

✂✃

Billy Dale Smith remembered well a very foggy day at the lake:

"We usually had a compass, but this particular day we didn't have one with us. We pointed the boat in the direction we needed to go, full throttle across the lake, couldn't see your fingers in front of your face. When we finally landed, we tried to figure out where we were. We were back at the boat dock where we started."

✂✃

Snow geese are found in other states, but are very rarely seen in Kentucky. Billy Dale Smith told about spotting these special birds one year:

"Snow geese were something you wanted to kill because they were so rare. One day there were two big snow geese and we were figuring on how we were going to get them in. They circled and we let them get away, kicking ourselves for not shooting at them. Lo and behold when we got back to the bank the game warden was there and asked us if we'd seen the whistling swans? We said 'Yep, we'd seen them.' We were really glad we hadn't taken our shot!"

Nana's Best Goose Dressing *by Shirley Smith*

2 frozen geese	1 lb. Pepperidge Farm stuffing mix
4 tbsp. salt	4 blades celery, diced
2 tbsp. white vinegar	2 eggs
2 lb. country sage sausage	Salt and pepper to taste
1/4 lb. butter	Lemon and water
1 large diced onion	

Wash and soak birds in vinegar and salt water for approximately two hours. Drain and dry thoroughly inside and out. Rub cavity with lemon.

Cook sausage and onion in butter until done. Combine stuffing mix, eggs, celery and sausage mixture well. Add water to moisten, then

add salt and pepper. Stir well. Stuff birds and baste with butter. Bake
at 350 degrees for approximately 3 to 4 hours based on the size of the
birds or until they are done.

Basketball Games

Billy Smith's father, Hal Smith, was a notable basketball player in his days
at Kirksey High School. In researching the family history, we came across
news accounts of his prowess on the court. The November 1929 issue of the
Echo, the high school newsletter, featured a full page on the Constitution of
the Kentucky High School Athletic Association, laying out the Articles of
Incorporation and opportunity for membership. The original Constitution
was adopted in 1917 and was apparently being reviewed by KHS. The
publication also included the following, excerpted from an article about
basketball:

> *"The K.H.S. Eagles are already soaring high into a sky of victory
> with five games to their credit out of six games with the best teams of the
> country. Hal Smith, known as "Al" is playing his second year with the
> Eagles. He is six feet in height and handles himself well. He is a hard fighter
> and has proven himself able to cope well with anyone playing center on the
> floor this season. Since he is a junior he has one more year with K.H.S".*

Hal's future brother-in-law, our Uncle Harvey, was also mentioned in the
article: "Harvey Story, the fastest man on the floor, is our running ace. In the
game with Brewers, he struck terror to the hearts of the Marshall basketeers
by his clever passing and his surprising ability to find the basket through a
jungle of guards."

The January 1930 issue of the *Echo*
reports: "Did you know that the Kirksey
Eagles have played eight games and won
seven of them? Did you know that those
eight games were played with the best
teams in this section of the country? Did

**Hal Smith holding the ball in the center with
Uncle Harvey seated at the far right.**

you know that Venable is getting better every day and that Hal Smith is one of the best ball players in Calloway County?"

While basketball was her dad's sport, Bettie Smith Stoll found that she liked baseball better:

"When I was little, the only way my big brother, Billy, would let me play ball with the boys would be if I agreed to be the hind catcher. I had my nose knocked out of place at least three times."

Following close on her heels were Bobbie Smith Bryant's attempts at playing softball:

"I played softball for several years, all through high school and several years afterward. I was the first baseman for a team over in Tri-City and usually played well, though I never could run very fast. The only time I regretted playing was when a batter and I collided at the base and I broke my nose. I never passed out, but I certainly understood the term 'seeing stars' from a whole new perspective!"

Bobbie (Smith) Bryant playing soft ball at Tri-City, 1982.

Josh Smith was also athletic:

"All through school I played basketball, football and baseball. I loved sports of all types. One year Dad was the assistant coach for baseball, and after every Little League game we'd always go to the Dairy Queen, win or lose. As I got into high school, I just played

Josh Smith playing football at Calloway County High School.

football. Even Nana and Pap made every game that I played in high school. One year when their friends Van and Gloria Rogers came for a visit from Overland Park, Kansas, they even came to see me play. One of my favorite memories was the year that my cousin, Suzannah Stoll, was a student at Murray State University. I could hear her yelling and screaming, cheering me on at every game.

    I don't ever remember playing in any sporting event that Dad wasn't there; he never missed a game that I know of. I know how tough that was for him as football always falls during his busiest time of the year."

Janae Smith playing volleyball.

Not to be outdone by her older brother, Janae Smith has become quite the ball player as well. Janae played softball at the Kirksey Ball Park for a few years, but when she was in the 7th grade, a conversation with a girlfriend gave her a new focus:

    "She was telling me how much fun she was having playing volleyball. It did sound fun, so I decided to try it, too. We had a good year and came in second that year. I'm still playing and we played really well during our second tournament this year. The more we play, the better we're getting."

Motor Sports

    The Kentucky State Fair began not long after the War of 1812, and many counties followed suit with their own local fairs. Showing cattle and hogs, prized quilts, vegetables, desserts and canned goods became the norm as families sought to compare their accomplishments to others. As time went by, farm equipment also took the stage as farmers competed with trucks and tractors to find out whose was the most powerful.

Billy Dale Smith was caught up in the excitement of tractor pulls and became a participant:

"When I was in high school, I was running around with a boy whose dad had a hot rod tractor. I'd always been interested in tractor pulls, and I started riding with him going around the state pulling his tractor. He built a new one and wanted to sell his old one, so I bought it. I'm proud I did; it was an economy class tractor, didn't cost too much, and I had the time to do it back then.

Billy Dale Smith with his hot-rod tractor, the Kirksey Critter.

Customized caricature design on the seat of the Kirksey Critter, painted by neighbor and friend, Randy Tucker.

I was thinking of a cute and interesting name, and I named it the Kirksey Critter. Randy Tucker painted the seat with a caricature, and Dale Sutherland helped me to keep the thing running. It always had plenty of power, but it had small tires. I did better on hard tracks rather than soft. With me being as a big as I am, I wasn't able to put much extra weight on it, so I had more trouble pulling on the soft tracks. One year I came in fifth in the state. When I got married, I had to give it up, but I still have the frame."

❦

Calloway County has been known since the Great Depression as the Used Car Capital of the World, and the Smith men took an early interest

A father and son project for Billy, Billy Dale and Josh, a 1949 Chevrolet pick up.

in restoring old cars. Billy Dale Smith remembered spending time with his young son, Josh:

"He began putting together model cars, and then began thinking about what he'd drive when he turned 16. He began talking about an old truck, and I thought it'd be a good project for us to do together. He did, too, and we began and worked on it for five years. We had to put it together and take it apart a hundred times. I burned him out I guess; money was tight and it would take a while to get the parts that we needed. My dad took an interest and, while he didn't do a lot of the work, what started as a father and son project ended as a son and father project as it became project for me and my dad, rather than me and my son.

After we were done with the truck, I showed it to one of the landlords we rented ground from. He had an old, rusted-out and ugly four-door car in his barn that he showed me. I told Dad about it and he said it sounded like the first car he'd ever driven. So we went back to look at it and sure enough it was like the one he'd driven, so Mom bought it for Dad."

Billy Smith picked up the story:

"After we moved from Little Rock, Ark., to Eddyville, Ky., Billy Dale called Shirley one day and said he had found a car that he thought was like the first car that I had purchased when I turned 16 and gotten my driver license. Mother asked him what kind and he said it was a four-door '51 Plymouth and it was in a tobacco barn that joined our farm at Kirksey, and that they wanted $500 for it. She told him to buy it and she gave it to me for my 60th birthday. We pulled it over to Billy Dale's farm shop and he had a young man working for him that knew quite a bit about body and mechanic work for cars.

Billy and Shirley attending Billy's 50th High School Reunion in 2005 in his remodeled 1951 Plymouth.

I was working in Eddyville, Ky., at the river terminal and on slow days, I learned to use the computer, as I had to get on the Internet to find new parts to restore the car. This was the time when I fell in love with computers and they have been my constant crutch for the last 12 years. This project took nearly three years to complete and cost a small fortune. However, I did come out with a beautifully restored 1951 Plymouth, just like the one I owned in 1953.

Billy Dale and our grandson, Josh, had also just restored a 1949 Chevrolet pick up truck that looks like a brand new one. Billy Dale and I showed the two vehicles at nearly all the car shows in a 100-mile radius for four to five years. It got to be pretty expensive and it got old after a few years. You would go to a car show in the summer and the temperature would be in the high 90's or low 100's. When you got to the show you had to pay a $20 to $25 entry fee, wipe off the car inside and out, sit in the sun and sweat for six to eight hours as people would come to view your car. After sweating and working most of the day, if you were lucky enough to place in the top three in your class, you would receive a $12 trophy to take home and set on a shelf. All they would be good for was to look at and wipe the dust off occasionally.

After getting back home and putting the car in garage, you had to wipe it down to get the bugs and dust off, and if we had a summer thunderstorm you had to raise the car up on a high lift and clean the bottom. I decided after four or five years that I could find something better to do on a hot summer day other than go to car shows and wipe on old cars.

I do want to say here that I really love my old car and a couple of times a year, Shirley and I will take it for a spin on a Sunday afternoon and go by the Dairy Queen in Murray and have a milkshake and talk about the good old days. I really love and appreciate Shirley for buying the car for me on my 60th birthday. It is exactly like the first one that I had—inside and out."

When Josh graduated from college, Billy Dale bought him a 1976 Corvette that Shirley's stepbrother (Bill David Wilson) wanted to sell. Josh still loves his Corvette and enjoys driving it. He hopes someday to restore it, too.

Josh Smith's 1976 Corvette.

CHAPTER IX

From the '50s to the '70s

*M*any things have affected the development of agriculture through the years: transportation, wars, immigration, education, and weather, to name a few. Although most residents of Calloway County are aware of the influence of farming on their community, many may not realize the significance.

Cover of Nation's Agriculture magazine, featuring the Billy and Shirley Smith family in 1966.

A November 1966 feature article on the Smith family in *Nation's Agriculture*, a national publication of the American Farm Bureau Federation, explains how Billy and Shirley Smith worked together in farming. "...Billy's dad owned a grocery store, thus Billy got a first hand view of the food business. Later, the family moved to the town of Kirksey, where Hal Smith established a general store. In the meantime, Billy spent summers on the nearby farm of his granddad, Sam Brewer. ... The youngster seemed to take naturally to livestock, so when he was 13, his granddad helped him buy a calf. This proved to be the spark that kindled his interest in farming. Three years later, the grandfather loaned Billy $1,000 to buy his first 40 acres of land. With this came a tobacco base of 1.2 acres. The next year, as a senior in high school, Billy had the land paid for through his success with tobacco and beef cattle."

Billy told the story this way:

Billy Smith and Charles Coleman sporting their FFA jackets. *Photo courtesy 1955 KHS Annual.*

"My first year at Kirksey was good. There was one special boy that became a personal and good friend, and today I still call him my best friend, Charles Coleman. We had a lot in common and dated together, ran around together and still visit and enjoy each other's company, 58 years later. There was a new Ag teacher that year at Kirksey, Harvey Ellis, who was 12 to 15 years older than the students were. I immediately became very interested in him and he in me. I joined the Future Farmers of America (FFA) organization and became part of my new school.

That summer, Dad helped me buy a motor bike and I could ride it to Papa Brewer's. I got my first calf for my FFA project and started helping Papa Brewer with his crops. I had to have a project in FFA and I rented ground from him and Papa Smith to grow corn and tobacco. In fall of 1955 I bought my first tractor, a VAC Case tractor with a tricycle front end and in the summer of 1956 I bought a 1955 red belly Ford tractor. This was to be my start to manhood. I enjoyed FFA, became an officer in my sophomore year, and became president the next year and in my senior year was state FFA president and got the honor of achieving the Kentucky State Farmer Award."

Meanwhile, Billy won two trophies for his tobacco display at the Kentucky State Fair and showed his beef cattle in FFA competition. Then came his first Farm Bureau honor, being named Calloway County King. One

Calloway County King and Queen, Billy Smith and Shelby Parker Suiter.

indication of his future as an innovator was Billy's decision to cure his tobacco in an easier and more efficient way by developing a labor-saving electrical curing process, the first of its kind. After his graduation from Kirksey High School, Billy attended Murray State College for one semester. Then he married Shirley, a legal secretary.

Billy recalled how they met:

Billy Smith with his green and white 1955 Chevrolet Bellaire.

"In the spring of 1955 during the high school regional basketball tournament, me, Charles Coleman and some other boys were out cruising and came across a few girls walking down the street and being boys, and they being girls, we picked them up and wound up taking two of them home. We asked about a date for Saturday night and they accepted. Saturday night came and I picked up Charles and proceeded to 606 Sycamore Street in Murray. On the way up to the house, Charles asked me which girl I wanted. I said, 'Why don't you get out and leave the front door open and open the back door? Whichever one gets in front is mine, and the one that gets in back is yours.' He said that sounded good to him.

That decision changed my life forever. Shirley got in the front and Jane got in the back. Shirley and I became quite fascinated with each other, and it was not long before we were going steady. I had dated a few girls in the past year, but none turned me on like this one. She was

Best friends Jane Vaughn and Shirley Chilcutt Smith.

Billy and Shirley in their dating years, celebrating Easter.

a junior and I was a senior when we first met. That fall I started to college, she was a senior in high school, and we just became closer. She was good looking and very smart—she got to helping me with my homework as I just did not take to college life. I wanted to get married and become a full-time farmer.

I got her a ring for Christmas and the week I bought the ring, I had a barn of tobacco to burn down and didn't have any insurance. Dad asked me what I was going to do and I said I didn't know, but that she was still going to get the ring if she would have it. She said yes. We had a good Christmas and both families were great and gave us all the support they could.

We were married in June and moved into the two back rooms over Dad's store and stayed there until the fall. Then we moved into a rented house, which was owned by G.W. Edmonds, a brother-in-law to John Cunningham. The house had only three rooms. One bedroom, kitchen, living room and two fireplaces and on the back porch a well with a bucket tied to a rope. Yes, that's right—no running water. And, if that

Billy and Shirley's wedding day, June 10, 1956 at Shirley's parents home at 606 Sycamore Street in Murray.

The first house Billy and Shirley lived in, owned by G. W. Edmunds, located on the Jim Washer Road in the Kirksey community.

wasn't enough, the bathroom was a small, one room house with a half moon on the door, about 25 yards from the back door of the larger house.

It was a cold winter; the fireplaces were really not fireplaces but open grates that burned coal. At night I would bring in two buckets of coal and set them on the hearth and we would take turns getting up to put coal on the fire as it was so cold that winter. When I would wake up and look out the window, the frost was on the inside of window and I would have to scrape it off to see how deep the snow was.

Shirley was working for State Sen. George Ed Overby and making good money as a secretary. I worked at the tobacco loose-leaf floor in January, February and March. I had bought a 40-acre farm when I was a senior in high school and I got an opportunity to buy another farm on the Kirksey Highway about 1½ miles north of Stella. The farm was 80 acres and gave us an opportunity to buy more Hereford cows. This house did not have indoor plumbing, but Shirley made me promise that I would put in running water and a bathroom, which we did. Billy Dale was born here as well as Bobbie.

Billy holding Billy Dale at the Burie Suiter farm stead.

We built a large chicken house with over a thousand layers. We had to gather eggs several times a day. One funny story was one day when Billy Dale was just over 1 year old, he went to the chicken house with me to pick up eggs. He was about half afraid of the hens, so I would let him stay in the egg packing room. When I came back with a basket of eggs, he was standing in the door and tossing eggs out into the house where the hens were. He would laugh out loud every time an egg would hit and bust."

Billy Dale Smith recalled:

"Yeah, when I was a little older, when we had those banty hens and roosters, they'd roost right above the door where you entered in the barn. Every day when you'd go in to collect eggs, the rooster would flog you. One day I took a broom and when the rooster came after me, I hit him. He looked like he was dead, but I guess he was just knocked out for a while. The next day he was up and running around again but I don't know that he ever flogged me again."

Billy Smith continued:

"We had to have running water 24 hours a day and lights on part of the night. If we could convince the hens that we had two days in a 24-hour period, they would lay two eggs in a day. We had to wash and grade the eggs to size and package them. Lynn Grove Egg Company would pick up eggs two times a week and deliver feed twice a week. The eggs had to be picked up several times a day, especially in the winter, or they would freeze. This was a lot of work and we got a chance to sell this farm for quite a bit more money than we had invested in it and we sold out the last day of November and promised to be out in 30 days.

We had to find a place to live, get rid of a chicken contract, find a place for

Billy Smith with his cattle at the Cain place.

50 head of cattle and a barn full of hay, and move in 30 days. We rented a place on the Penny Highway and moved the family there. We moved the cattle, some to Papa Smith's farm and the rest to Papa Brewer's farm. We moved the hay and ear corn to both farms. Shirley said if I did her that way again she would leave me and take the kids with her.

During this time I had also become a substitute rural mail carrier. The winter of 1959/1960 was bad. It snowed all winter, but the worst was to come in March, when we had over 22 inches of snow. I worked with Zane Coleman who was the regular rural mail carrier. We would ride with each other and get out to put mail in the mail boxes; Zane split his salary with me for helping him. This was a big boost to our income. In April that year, Papa Brewer and I went to the woods in the third week of April and shoveled the snow off a spot for a plant bed so we could plant a tobacco crop. Plant beds were about a month late that year, but we still made a good crop of tobacco.

Papa Brewer wanted to buy a farm at Penny, and I told him I would try to buy his farm that bordered my first 40-acre farm. We stored our furniture in the old house that R.W. Blakley had emptied as he had just built a new house and we moved in with Mama and Papa Brewer. They finally got the farm at Penny purchased and moved and then we got our furniture back. I applied for a loan to buy the farm from Prudential Life Insurance Company and they loaned me $10,000, but I still needed $3,000. I asked Papa Smith if he would loan this amount to me and he said he would.

I had bought some steers from Audrey Simmons who ran the Murray Stock Yards and made good money feeding them for 90 days. I thought I would double the number and make twice as much in the next three to four months. Guess what? I bought the steers and put them on feed and pasture, they cost a few dollars more than the last ones, but no one told me the price might go down. It did. Not just a dollar or two per 100 pounds, but $15 per pound. I lost more than twice as much on this bunch as I had made on the first ones.

If this wasn't bad enough, as I was working in public work, I'd left

Billy Smith with his prize Hereford.

Shirley with the kids on the farm. This was probably the most unhappy time for her. She did not like the isolation of the farm. We had a gravel road and most days the only traffic was the milk man and the mail man. She was not used to working with cattle and enjoyed being around people more than cows.

The cows would get out and someone would call her and she had to get me to come home and round them up. One day they got out and that night our neighbors, John Cunningham and G. W. Edmonds, came up and told me that our cows had got into one of their corn fields and ate the entire field of young corn plants. The next morning I went to see for myself and found where they had got out and, sure enough, they had eaten most all the plants.

The corn was just a little under knee-high and it looked like they had just gone down every row and bitten off every plant, just above the ground. G.W. and I talked and I told them that if the corn did not grow out and make a good crop, I would pay them in the fall after the harvest. To all of our surprise, the corn did

Hereford cattle checking out the farm at the Cain place.

grow out and John and G. W. said that the field made the best corn crop they had ever harvested there.

I called Audrey Simmons that summer and had him sell all of my cattle. This was a relief for Shirley that she did not have to worry about them bothering the neighbors any more and I did not have to get up in the winter at 5 a.m. and feed them in the cold before I went to work. When we sold out, we had a herd of 70 registered brood cows and calves.

Two years later Papa Smith told me he thought I should pay back the money I owed him. I had to go to the bank and borrow it, which would have been hard if not for Harvey Ellis being my banker. He had left his job at the school system and was now the agriculture loan officer at People's Bank. Thank God for little things."

❧❦

Billy has strong feelings for Harvey Ellis and shared:

"He was my lifeline at the bank for my first 20 years of married life. He had a lot of confidence in me and would loan me money when I thought he would surely turn me down. He stayed with me until early 1970s when Shirley and I wanted to open The Showcase, a bridal shop. That is when he sent us to see Mr. Doran, the president of People's Bank. Much to our surprise and to our liking, he said okay and never did turn us down for any request we made.

There was one time, though, when I thought he was going to. This was in the mid to late 1970s when we were having high inflation and our neighbor whose property adjoined ours, R. W. Blakley, was ready to sell his farm. On Labor Day weekend he came over and told us that he was going to sell the farm and, as I had asked him when he sold out to give me first chance, he did what he promised, saying now is the time he wanted to sell. I asked how much he wanted for it and he told me. I told him he wanted way too much and before I could say anything else, he said okay, there is another person who will buy it for this price. I said now wait a minute, let me talk to the banker in the morning. He interrupted me and said if I wanted the farm for me to give him a check and he would hold it till noon the next day.

H. Glen Doran and Harvey Ellis of Peoples Bank. *Photo courtesy of Hutson Chemical Co. marketing brochure.*

Well, I had less than a $100 in the bank and the check I wrote was for $90,000. I told him to wait until after lunch to take it to the bank and he said he would wait till 12 noon. Then I had to go in the house and tell Shirley what I had done.

This was the first and last cold check I ever wrote. I was standing at the front of the bank door, five minutes before 8:00 a.m. the next morning. The doors were unlocked and I went in, straight to Mr. Doran's office. I met him coming down the hall with a cup of coffee and he offered me one and said come on in. We chatted for a few minutes and I told him what I had done the previous day. He said, 'What?' and I told him again.

He started to lecture me and tell me the many reasons that I should not have done a thing like that. After about an hour I interrupted him and said if you are not going to loan me the money I have just three hours to raise it and I will have to go across the Court Square and talk to the people at the Bank of Murray. He raised up and nearly came out of his seat and pointed his finger at me from across his desk and said, 'I'm going to loan you the money, but don't you ever do me this way again!' I apologized profusely and said I would not and I never did, nor will I ever again do something like that to him or to any one else.

To this day I still think that Mr. Doran is the greatest man and banker I have ever known. We talked until noon and at about one minute 'til 12, in walked Mr. Blakley with my check to deposit. Mr. Doran picked up the phone and talked to the teller and the teller did not even look up when Mr. Blakley was at the window cashing his check. I thanked Mr. Doran and went home to have lunch, quite relieved.

Just a few years later when the financial situation got better, Shirley had already built The Showcase and was wanting to expand

The original Showcase, opened in 1973 on Highway 121 in Murray.

the building she was in. He agreed to loan her the money. I still give Harvey Ellis and especially Mr. Doran credit for what Shirley and I have accomplished. They furnished the money and Shirley and I furnished the desire, labor and time."

❦

Shirley's training and experience as a secretary came in handy with work on the farm. She proved an especially adept hand at the farm figuring and bookkeeping. And when it came to doing the regular farm chores, she jumped right in along with her husband. In spite of their both being city kids at the start, they made a real farm team.

The Smiths became involved in Farm Bureau activities. Soon, Billy was asked to sit in on a county board of director's meeting. The *Nation's Agriculture* article notes that Billy was eventually named president of the Calloway County Farm Bureau and held the post for two years. During that time, he and Shirley were instrumental in getting the county young people's program up and running.

As Billy Smith noted:

"We had a lot of encouragement in Farm Bureau. We went with Noble and Jonnie Cox to Chicago to attend the American Farm Bureau convention and returned on the train. This was our very first train ride. Jonnie and Noble were an older couple that lived across the street from Mother and Dad when they lived at the store in Kirksey. Noble was always trying to help Shirley and me to become somebody. They were

FFA letterhead featuring Billy Smith as President.

actively involved in the Farm Bureau and after I bought a car and needed insurance they got me as a Farm Bureau insurance customer as well as getting us both involved in Farm Bureau activities.

When I received the American Farmer Degree in 1957 we went back to Kansas City to receive it. Shirley was pregnant at that time and while we were there she bought her first trimester tops to wear when she started to show. This was also our first time to see a U.S. president in person. President Truman was the guest speaker one day and Paul Harvey was speaker the next day. Another big deal for a country boy and girl!"

American Farm Bureau's Young Peoples Committee chairman, Billy Smith.

Billy served on the American Young People's Committee for two years and in 1964 was chosen as the chairman. Later that year he was named the winner of the Jaycee's Distinguished Service Award for Calloway County. In 1966 he served on the state Farm Bureau Board of Directors once again. As president of the American Farm Bureau Young People's Committee, Billy was automatically a member of the American Farm Bureau board of directors. This was a great experience as he learned a lot and made many great friends during those years. In 1966 he served on the Kentucky State Farm Bureau board of directors again.

Billy Smith told about a life-changing time in the fall of 1959:

"On a Sunday afternoon we wanted to go get an ice cream cone and we could not scrape up enough nickels, dimes and quarters to buy the four of us ice cream at the Dairy Dip. That was the day that I decided that I was going to find something else to do to make a living so we could enjoy our lives as a family.

I went to General Tire in Mayfield and applied for a job. I was hired on as a fork truck driver and was to report to work at 3:30 p.m. the next day. When I went in to punch the clock there was a note on my card that said I needed to report to the office. I went and they told me they were sorry but they could not hire me because I had an extra vertebra in my back, making 13 on each side. I was very disappointed and went to see Dr. Charles Clark, our family doctor. He made me an appointment in Memphis to see a specialist and Shirley and I went to Memphis on December 26. The doctor examined me and took ex-rays, and said that they were right, that I did have 13 vertebras in my back. He said that it would not be a problem for me and to go home and get back to work. Even with this physician's note, General Tire would still not hire me.

Hamp Brooks was by then the Ag teacher at Kirksey and was teaching a night course for young farmers in the area, one night a week. I asked him about getting a job somewhere and he said that Dan Hutson was looking for someone to replace Lester Nanny who was running his office at the fertilizer plant. I was in Mr. Hutson's office the next morning. He hired me for $47.50 per week.

I was working at the tobacco

Billy working at Hutson's on Railroad Avenue in Murray located at the old depot.

Hutson's river terminal located at the Tennessee River at Kentucky Lake. *Photo courtesy Hutson Chemical Company brochure.*

floor and he said to come to work when their work was over. I went to work for Hutson Chemical Company on March 30, 1960, and stayed with Mr. Hutson until December 20, 1990. He was very good to me, and I always thought he was paying me just enough to keep me from going somewhere else. I progressed with Hutson's, becoming an executive at Hutson Company and president of Kenlake International. Mr. Hutson told me he would back any thing I did, but not to make the same mistake twice. When I went to work for Hutson, they had less than $1 million in sales. When I left 30 years later, we had sales of over $40 million.

After the first 10 years, and in the beginning of 1960, my responsibilities were mainly in the office and helping all around the plant. In the early 1970s the agricultural market really took off. I had just started sitting in on talks with Mr. Hutson and our suppliers. I enjoyed this type of work and really enjoyed selling railcars. I began to broker a few barges. We started hiring people to help and these guys and gals all became a tremendous force in the fertilizer business. Over the years we built four river terminals in our expansion and two inland rail terminals. Some of the people that we hired are still some of my closest friends today.

Sometime in the early 1970s, Hutson Chemical Corporation formed Kenlake International and this gave us the opportunity to buy and sell in the international markets. This was the highlight of my tenure with Hutson's as it gave me the chance to travel overseas and to trade, buy and sell internationally. It is a lot of fun when everybody is making money."

CHAPTER X

From the '70s to Today

*B*illy Smith, followed by Billy Dale and Josh, picked up the narration to bring the story into current times.

Billy Smith remembered:

"Billy Dale always wanted to farm, and he was doing a man's day of work when he was an early teenager. He started helping with the farming before he ever got in high school. Some time in the early 1970s Lubie Parrish and his two sons, Rob Edd and Elvin Lee, asked me if Billy Dale and I would want to form a partnership and rent the Joe Dunn farm. We had just bought a new Case self-propelled combine and they had one just like it. We farmed our land, they farmed their land, and we farmed the 300 acres at the Dunn farm together.

Billy Dale Smith in 1976.

Lubie was working at the Ryan Milk Plant as a deliveryman and I was working at Hutson. Reba Faye was running their hamburger restaurant and Shirley opened The Showcase in 1972. The boys were in school and we would all work at night and weekends together. This lasted until about 1980 when we lost the Dunn Farm to the government Conservation Reserve Program.

Combining with the Smith and Parrish families in the mid 1970s.

While we worked at Mr. Dunn's farm cutting wheat, we'd be breaking and working the ground to plant soybeans behind it. Before we could break the ground, the wheat was so strong that we'd have to burn it off. We had finished cutting the wheat one Saturday afternoon, just before dark. Shirley and Reba brought our supper to us in the field. Just after dark, we set the straw on fire to burn off the field so we could disc the field and plant beans. We tied grass sacks that had been soaked in diesel fuel behind a couple of pick up trucks and set them on fire and proceeded to drag the sacks around the 80-acre field. The straw caught on fire and started to burn big time. We had people coming from as far as Benton, Mayfield and Murray to see what was burning and to help put it out. The next day the boys that had been on the tractors were solid black from the smoke and fires.

As Lubie and I were working five to six days a week, Saturday and Sunday were the only time we could farm and so on the weekends we put in two good 24-hour days. One other weekend in mid-June we were cutting wheat and trying to plant soybeans behind the wheat. This was before there was well-built no-till equipment. Someone called the rescue squad and they came and tried to put the fire out, all the while we were telling them we were just burning off the field. Quite an exciting time for country boys

The Parrish family worked in partnership with the Smith family during the 1970s.

trying to work. However, we did start calling the rescue squads before we set other fires.

We usually would try to work the entire weekend (both day and night). If we got where we just had to sleep a short time we would get in the back of one of the pick-up trucks and take a short nap. One Sunday morning Lubie found me sitting on my 8000 Ford tractor with the disc behind it, sound asleep, with my foot on the clutch and the motor running wide open. He was afraid to try to get to me as I might wake up and my foot would come off the accelerator. He threw dirt clods at me until he finally hit me and woke me up. I don't how long I had been asleep but I shut the tractor down and got off and took a nap.

As the Parrishes and the Smiths were farming together in their small partnership, both families decided to purchase a cabin on the Kentucky Lake at Springville, Tennessee, together. We all enjoyed several years relaxing and boating on the lake in the summertime. It was a good place to unwind when we could find time.

After several years we decided to disband the partnership with the Parrish family. Lubie retired from his milk route and he and Reba ran the hamburger restaurant for several years. Their boys took over their farm and Billy Dale took most of the responsibility for our farm when he graduated from high school, as I was working and traveling for Hutson's. Shirley operated The Showcase and I worked at Huston's, all during the high interest rates of the 1980s. Billy Dale continues to farm and bought out the partnership that we had on the farm and became a full-time farmer in 1990."

Billy Dale Smith picked up the story:

"When we were first farming, and before we had big fuel tanks to fill up our tractors and other machinery; diesel fuel was around 35 cents a gallon. In the 1970 to 1974 time period, every day we'd go to Martin Oil with five gallon fuel cans and we'd have to fill them all up, and then go back to the farm where the tractors were and use funnels to fill up the tractors. When we got the first 100-gallon storage tank with a pump, we thought we were big-time farmers because we could pull the tractors up

to the tank and fill them up. Today the tractors hold 80 to 100 gallons each and the road tractors hold up to 200 gallons each. Farm storage fuel tanks today are over 3,000 gallons."

❦

Josh Smith also recalled:

Workers hanging tobacco in the barn at Smith Farms.

"I remember the very first check I ever made working in tobacco. Our neighbor, Timmy Falwell, was running tobacco in at the Palmer place. Mr. Palmer had called Dad to see if anyone could come over and run the top tier. I was probably 9 or 10 at the time and old enough to know that if you're in the top beams you've got to hold on or risk getting hurt. I was also old enough to know that I needed to work really hard as I was working for someone other than family. I was just big enough to spread my legs to touch both sides of the rails where we were running in the tobacco.

I was glad that I was in the very top tier as you don't have to handle every piece as it comes in. I was getting about every fourth or fifth stick. It was a one-acre barn and took about an hour of work. I remember when I got the check, Mom made a photo copy of it and Dad hung it in the office. It was my very first work check, for a whopping $7.

❦

When I was in high school, we were at Rob Edd's place and I of course knew everything there was to know about farming. I was supposed to be setting up the auger and David was coming with the truck. Dad was *trying to tell me how to set it up, but I thought my way was better than his, and I told him that if he wanted it done that way that he'd have to do it. He was probably getting fed up with my know-it-all demeanor and said, 'Come on out here. ... I'll put you on the ground or we'll do it your way.'*

Well, I laughed in my head, as here I am: I'm 17 and I play football, so I'm thinking I can take him out, nothing flat. I charged after him, planning to tackle him, pick him up, pass him over my shoulder and put him on the ground. When I charged, he sidestepped me. My momentum was going so fast that I fell face and fists first into the gravel. Of course now I'm mad. I go after him again, now he's smiling. This time he grabs me by the shoulders, spins me, not once, but twice, and slings me on the ground. He said do you still want to fight or do you want to do it my way? I told him it would be good to do it his way as I didn't know that my way would work all that well after all. To this day, if he wants to do it his way, we'll do it his way. It's not worth it!"

❦

Billy Dale Smith shared more memories:

"During the early 1980s there came a time that we farmers were being encouraged to diversify, to get away from tobacco production. The first year was with bell peppers. Supposedly there was a co-op to start up over in Christian County. Well, I got crossways with the co-op over transportation and having to buy boxes for shipping and other things that just didn't work right. So here I sit with five acres of peppers and nowhere to send them.

Harvest time rolled around and we were hauling peppers to Tennessee so they could ship them to Chicago. We were trying

Diversifying the crops at Smith Farms in the 1980s. This picture features red peppers being loaded for shipping.

to sell them in roadside stands by the crateful. One man was processing in Calloway County and said he wanted all he could get. We sent him a two-ton truck load and a pickup truck full where he would clean, sort and size them before shipping. After he had supposedly processed them and it was time for me to get a check, he'd only processed about 20 crates. He said he'd thrown the rest out into a compost pile. I wasn't real happy about that and that was the last time I shipped to him.

Diversified crop of green beans being shipped to market.

After that experience, I decided I wasn't going to grow peppers any more. But the next year there was a factory down south that had a receiving station that was buying pimento peppers, so instead of growing five acres I decide to grow one acre. That worked out decent enough, and though I didn't make much money, I was able to cover the cost, so we did it again for one more year. It seemed like the faster we could unload them, the more they'd take for their cannery.

Something I learned the first year—we had insurance on peppers and that was a Godsend. Peppers can get damaged real easy with sun scalding or by breaking off with high winds. The insurance paid off every year that we had peppers because we had some kind of damage each time.

After three years of experimenting with produce, I decided that there were more crooks in the produce market than in the tobacco market. So, I decided that I'd rather use everything I had to grow tobacco rather than experiment with peppers, but it was a good experience."

Josh Smith continued the story:

"When Dad had that first pepper patch, trying to diversify his crop, his crop was just behind the house and I was too little to pick peppers. The guys that picked peppers would put them into a basket and then bring them to the dump truck at the barn. My job was to sit in the dump truck, and look through the peppers to be sure they weren't messed up. If they looked gross, I was to throw them out. Being the lively young man *that I was, I'd look at the peppers and if they were bad, I'd throw them at the person who'd brought them, and tell them not to bring any more bad ones. They finally found that to be irritating and began to toss them back at me!"*

❧❧

Billy Dale Smith told about changes in the labor force:

Billy Dale Smith's first car, a 1976 Mercury Cougar.

"Back when I was going to school we were always wanting to get out of school to go to work. We wanted to make money to buy a car, put gas in the car, etc. It was never a problem to find help to work in tobacco, there was always plenty of help. I guess I remember $3 per hour was the price we paid for workers then. We hauled hay with a crew of three to five boys for 15 cents a bale and we'd haul about 2,500 to 3,000 bales a day. Help was always easy to get, even through the 70's and early 80's. Then, as the mid-80's came around, it was hard to get anybody to help. I remember going to work some days and only having me and one other person to work—cutting took forever. I began experimenting in the late 80's with getting migrant help. I went with another farmer to get the help we needed.

I had always worried when I was in high school that I should have taken Spanish because I knew someday I might need migrant help. But back then, the closest migrant workers were in Illinois working in orchards, so I didn't do it. I went through a broker in Texas to get workers here and that seemed to work well. It has evolved today that I couldn't do the work without them as you can't get anyone else to do the manual labor every day like they do.

H2A migrant workers provide much of the labor at Smith Farms.

Sometimes I get mad when I think about it. In my hey-day I could do the work twice as fast as they do it today, but then I realize that we grow tobacco twice as big now as we did back then and the Mexicans are not built physically as we are. The biggest problem we have is going through the U.S. government in how we have to qualify to work them. It would be a lot better if we could just work our relationship between me as the employer and them as the worker."

Billy Dale continued:

"*There's a lot to environmental regulations on the farm today—the record keeping that we have to do, keeping up with the amount of chemical, where it is has been applied, the wind direction, the temperature, who manufactures it, what the actual chemical is, what happens in case someone gets hurt or you have to go to the hospital. A lot of scrutiny is given to state and federal farm regulations, from environmental concerns and the toxicity of chemicals to OSHA regulations. Everything on the farm is potentially dangerous from chemicals, animals, machinery; anything can go wrong in a split second. The biggest danger is carelessness or forgetfulness.*

"*These regulations are a full-time job for a manager—keeping chemical records for EPA, truck records for DOT, labor-H2a program (immigration and wage and hour). This doesn't include regular financing and record keeping, which also have to be done and done well. In school I thought farmers didn't have to know anything, they just had to work. Was I ever wrong."*

Preparing to strip tobacco at Smith Farms.

The Smith Women and *The Showcase*

Billy and Shirley Smith expanded into the retail world in 1972, buying a lot zoned for business on Highway 121 North in Murray and having a building constructed to house *The Showcase*—a shop for formal and bridal fashions. When the building was almost finished, the pair took the two-ton farm truck and Billy's cousin, Sharon Story Brown, and headed to St. Louis to buy shop fixtures.

Billy Smith remembered getting started:

Shirley's Showcase after the addition was added in 1983. The shop was sold to new owners in 1990 when Shirley was diagnosed with and treated for breast cancer. Upon recovering, she and Billy moved to Overland Park, Kansas for Billy to begin a new position with a new company.

"Sharon had agreed to help Shirley operate The Showcase and Shirley wanted her to go with us and help pick out the fixtures: glass shelving, office equipment and everything that it took to operate a business. We bought eight freestanding glass and steel showcase islands along with several hundred feet of four-foot glass shelves and brackets to bolt them onto the walls. Junior Cleaver had built Shirley a round floor display stand with a turntable to attach a mannequin onto, and this became the focal point for the shop as the mannequin was always dressed in a beautiful wedding gown and veil and had a bright spotlight shining on it at all times.

We also had to buy office equipment that included a desk, two chairs, safe, filing cabinet, cash register, adding machine, and calculator. We purchased several

Sharon Story Brown was the first employee of The Showcase. She is a first cousin of Billy Smith.

hundred dress hangers and several dress racks, loaded all the above on the truck and threw a tarp over it and drove back to Murray, all in one very long day.

The center attraction of The Showcase was the bride mannequin which was highlighted with a spotlight and rotated to show all sides of the displayed wedding gown.

The Showcase started buying merchandise about six months before the store was ready to open. We had never been to a wholesale market before and found out that we could not just walk in and start ordering. I took my Hutson's business card and used it to get into the shows and then we would use The Showcase name and tax number to purchase the items we wanted. We gave Mr. Doran's name and telephone number at the Peoples Bank for credit references, and our home address for the companies to ship to.

We had the merchandise shipped to our house on the Kirksey Highway where we stored it in the living room and in the garage. When the building was completed, we took the merchandise to the store and put it on display. We began to order more as we had a very good grand opening celebration and it looked like the store was going to have to have more items to sell.

Modeling the fashions of the day were employees Jo Reeder and Martha Paschall and The Showcase owner, Shirley Smith.

Bobbie Smith models one of the formals at *The Showcase* in 1973.

 I especially liked going to market with Shirley and purchasing in large lots. I really enjoyed helping her in buying wedding gowns, bridesmaids and mother's gowns, prom and other formal dresses. We had to go to different types of markets for gifts, and this was always a joy as we could buy wholesale items that we had always wanted.

 It soon became apparent that this business was bigger than the all of us, and Shirley had to start hiring

At 23 years of age, Bobbie Smith moved to Hopkinsville, Ky. in 1983 and opened her own store, The Showcase, located at 16th and Clay Streets. The store closed in 1990 when Bobbie moved to Shelbyville, Ky. to begin a new career.

several more women to help. The shop grew and the work expanded from just selling and alterations to marketing and preparing for bridal and prom fashion shows that we conducted all across west Kentucky and west Tennessee.

Bobbie was only 13 when the shop opened and she worked after school and on the weekends all through her high school years. This experience provided an open door for her, and at the tender age of 23, she too opened her own shop in Hopkinsville. Both Shirley and Bobbie retired from their respective bridal businesses, Shirley in 1989 and Bobbie in 1990."

AFTERWORD

*T*he landscape of our forefathers is changing rapidly as the Smith family of Calloway County continues to make a living from the rich soil of the Jackson Purchase. For two full centuries farming in west Kentucky has been our way of life.

From the late 1700s to the dawn of the 21st century, not much changed in farming, particularly in the cultivation of tobacco. Yet we now realize that the tradition of farming as livelihood will be very different for generations to come.

As keepers of the land, we can't help but marvel at the amazing evolution of farming as a result of technological advances. And just as in the past, changes in state and federal laws as well as the court of public opinion have affected the way tobacco farming is viewed and supported.

With a desire to leave a legacy of love and a deep rooted sense of place, we present our collection of family stories and shared memories, intertwined with the local history and culture that pulses through our veins.

There have been a number of notable and newsworthy occurrences through the years involving members of the Smith family. Following are a few of them.

- In 1957, Billy Smith and several classmates were treated to a dinner sponsored by Herman K. Ellis for being outstanding corn yield growers in juvenile and adult classes. R. Pierce McDougall was top grower with 124.27-bushel average on 17 acres. Other high yield winners were Dr. A H. Kopperud, Albert Wilson, Charles Outland, Larry Suiter, Robert Craig and Bobby Bazzell.

- Billy Smith recalled one big high school project where he and other students set up displays at both the Kentucky State Fair and the Mid South Fair in Memphis.

Billy Smith receiving his American Farmer Degree at the National FFA Convention in Kansas City, Kansas in 1958.

"The display was named Tobacco and Its Products. We would dig up the plants and put them in tubs to keep them alive, taking tobacco in all stages of growth and show how the crop developed over the year. We also had products made from tobacco, such as cigarettes, plug tobacco, snuff, dark fired cigars, chewing tobacco and many brands of each. We would load up a two-ton truck late in the afternoon and into the evening and leave Kirksey about 10 p.m. and drive all night to Louisville. This was before the four-lane highways were built. We would go through Hopkinsville, Bowling Green and then north to Louisville. I remember my first trip to Louisville. When we loaded up, three of us sat in the cab and three rode in back. I was one of those in the back. Just as we were to leave, Mr. Ellis took a dark fired cigar and cut it into 3 pieces and told the three of us to chew it like chewing tobacco. He said we could spit it out the back of the truck. Being as it was my first experience at chewing, I think I chewed it like chewing gum. I was deathly sick before we got to Hopkinsville. I vomited out over the back of truck until we got to Bowling Green, about a two-hour drive. I have never been as sick as I was that night. I have never chewed tobacco since.We got to the fairgrounds around daylight and got into the building and set up our display. We also had the fathers of each of the boys on the trip to donate sticks of green tobacco, right out of the field, and we entered them in the different classes for green tobacco. The Kirksey FFA Chapter won over $1,000 in prize money and many blue ribbons. We got quite a bit of recognition for this trip. In about two or three weeks we carried the same display and tobacco to the Mid South Fair in Memphis. We had about the same results in Memphis.

- In 1965 The Kentucky Farm Bureau featured the Smith Family in the *Kentucky Farm Bureau News*, its monthly newsletter. The front page article featured the Smiths in their living room and was written as a national feature story as Billy had been named the chairman of the American Farm Bureau Young People's Committee.

1966 Nation's Agriculture monthly magazine article featuring the Smith family.

- Another feature article about the Smiths was in the November 1966 *Nation's Agriculture*, the American Farm Bureau Federation's monthly magazine. This three-page spread featured photos of the Smiths at their farm in Kirksey and the article described their farming efforts in terms of being a partnership.

Kentucky farm Bureau News article featuring the Smith Family in 1965.

As noted earlier, Billy Dale Smith spent a good deal of time in his youth pulling his hot rod tractor. He shared the story from the evening when a news reporter was on hand and shot the accompanying picture.

"I was mashing on the accelerator trying to get as much traction as I could. I pressed the pedal so hard that I broke

Billy Dale Smith shown in the local newspaper with his hot rod tractor, the Kirksey Critter.

the linkage going to the carburetor. That night, there wasn't a welder in sight, though normally there was. I had to tie a string onto the carburetor to use as a throttle and I found it difficult to pull the string, steer the tractor and keep everything under control. When I got the newspaper the next day, the article said something about a contraption that ran at the pull. I had to look up in the dictionary to see what contraption meant. It said it was something that would barely run. Guess that was a pretty accurate description that night."

The Murray Area Vocational Center offers additional courses for young adult farmers in which Billy Dale Smith participates.

Pictured left to right: Area Farmers, Tripp Furches, Mark Paschall, and Billy Dale Smith talking with David Riley, Calloway County ASCS at a recent young and adult farmer class at Murray Area Vocational Center. Other adult farmer classes are scheduled for this week with the New Concord Class meeting on Tuesday, Nov. 8 at the Lynn Grove Class meeting on Thursday, Nov. 10 at 7 p.m. The 1988 USDA Disaster Program and Multi-Peril Crop Insurance will be discussed at both of the classes. All interested area farmers are encouraged to attend. Johnnie Stockdale, Vocational Agriculture Teacher may be contacted at 753-1870 if you are interested in this years program.

- Billy Dale Smith has followed in his father's footsteps through the years, taking advantage of educational courses that have been offered in the community to

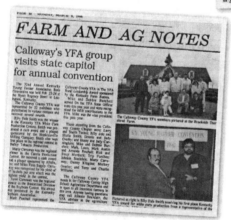

FARM AND AG NOTES

Calloway's YFA group visits state capitol for annual convention

Ky. YFA Convention recognizes winners in state Agriculture

Billy Dale Smith participated in the Young Farmers Association's annual farm convention.

Billy Dale Smith wins an award for white corn production in 1990.

keep up with developments in farming as well as best practices. In the three photos here, Billy Dale is recognized in 1988 and 1989 for taking part in the courses and again in 1990 with a first place award for the production of white corn.

- Shirley Smith learned a lot about farming from the family she married into; and in turn, the family learned a lot from her. In early 1990 Shirley learned that she had breast cancer. After a radical mastectomy and chemotherapy, she was inspired to help others by writing a book about her experiences during this turbulent and emotional time. Her book, *Time To Behold: Triumph Over Tragedy by Faith, Prayers and a Positive Attitude* was published in 1993. This inspirational book continues to encourage others who are faced with the uncertainties of life.

Shirley (Chilcutt) Smith becomes an author in 1994 with her first book, *A Time to Behold*.

During an extremely dry summer in 1999, Lt. Governor Steve Henry came to west Kentucky to see the drought damage. Billy Dale recalled:

"The county judge executive called to see if he could bring him out to our farm to see our crop. We had a good meeting— talked with him about how we irrigated some of our crops and the costs associated with doing so. We also talked about what we were expecting the crop to make and the losses we thought we were going to incur due to the weather. The local newspaper was

Lt. Governor Steve Henry visited Calloway County in 1999 and met with Billy Dale Smith on the farm.

following him around that day and so we had a small story in the local paper about his visit.

• Billy remembered another official visit:

"In the late fall of 2006 I got a phone call from Wayne Hunt of Hopkinsville, Ky., owner and manager of Agri-Power, Agri-Chem and Agri Port Terminal. He asked if we knew anyone that would host a breakfast for the Kentucky governor and lieutenant governor as they were making a campaign sweep through the western part of the state. I asked Billy Dale and he thought it would be a good thing for us to do. Gov. Fletcher and Lt. Gov. Robbie Rudolph came to Smith Farms as our guests along with about 60 other

Republican Governor Ernie Fletcher made a visit to Smith Farms on his campaign tour in 2007. Featured here are the Governor, Billy Dale and Billy Smith.

people from west Kentucky for a campaign rally that November. They were very pleased with the crowd and seemed to enjoy their tour of the farm as well as the country ham breakfast that was catered by the Kirksey Store. The governor seemed especially interested in the showroom where we have the three antique cars, especially the 1951 Plymouth. He said that his father and mother had one

During the Governor's visit around 50 local residents visited Smith farm for the campaign rally.

just like it when he was a young teenager. He seemed impressed with the whole farm layout and made a nice speech before leaving to move on to Murray for a public event."

- In 2006 Billy and Billy Dale Smith made an amazing trip to Antarctica, the only continent that Billy had not visited. On the way there, they stopped in Buenos Aires and spent about 36 hours touring a rich farming area

Russian tour vessel used by Billy and Billy Dale on their visit to Antarctica.

some 200 to 300 miles away. Billy provided an overview:

"We got a good view of how they grow soybeans, corn and other crops. They do a really good job as they get to use the knowledge, fertilizer, chemicals and hybrid seed that were discovered and proven in the U.S. several years ago. On the way back we stopped in Santiago, Chile, and spent about 36 hours touring their agricultural areas. They are doing an excellent job growing grapes, and I buy their grapes in the grocery stores as I think they are the best grapes that are produced anywhere in the world. Also they have a fairly new wine industry and are making a very good red wine and shipping it to the U.S."

City scene from Santiago, Chile when Billy and Billy Dale toured in 2006.

- Billy Dale talked about their visit at a farm tour in Argentina:

  "They have the same concerns that we have, and it helped me to see their crops and how they operate. I'd like to do these tours more often; it would really help us in marketing our products.

Soybean field in Argentina when Billy and Billy Dale toured there.

February down there is the same kind of weather that we have here in August. It's a critical time for growing their crops, and they have a lot of dry pockets down there. Traders at the Chicago Board of Trade wait to see what their growing season is producing before they set their prices. Knowing first hand about how things are going down there can help us sell and market our crops at a better price."

- Playing host to government officials and working with elected officials continues to be part of the Smith family's work. In 2008 a group of west Kentucky farmers met with the state representative from Graves County. Billy Dale reports:

  "He asked us to come to Frankfort and testify before the state Agriculture Committee and talk with them about our concerns with the H2A program, the immigrant worker program. Our main concerns were the bureaucratic red tape and how the government determines

In 2008 Billy Dale Smith and other farmers worked with elected officials to discuss the H2A migrant worker program.

the increase in wages. After we got up there and talked to them, I learned that a few of the representatives had agriculture backgrounds and some even owned their own farms. A few of them had used H2A program also. As far as knowing whether it helped any, I don't know yet, I hope it did. It was a good experience for me as it gave me a chance to see how our system of government works and be part of making something happen on issues that are important to me and our farm."

- In 2008 Josh's family was featured in the Murray State University magazine, noting Missy's recently published book, *I Choose to be Happy: A School Shooting Survivor's Triumph Over Tragedy*. Missy was a victim of a tragic school shooting at a Paducah high school in 1997. She continues to speak across the country, recounting her story of forgiveness as

Missy (Jenkins) Smith's biography, *I Choose to be Happy: A School Shooting Survivor's Triumph Over Tragedy*.

Josh Smith's family featured in the Murray State University magazine in 2008.

she copes with the results of the shooting. She is dedicated to helping children and youngsters as they face bullying and other pressures during their school and life experiences. Missy's book is available at www.missyjenkins.com.

- In 2011, Smith Farms was featured in a network-quality documentary on dark-fired tobacco. Produced by Michael Breeding MEDIA, the documentary features Billy Dale Smith and his father, Billy Smith, reflecing upon the age-old and often forgotten farming culture of dark-fired tobacco. The film vividly shows life on a modern tobacco farm while explaining the history and processes of this little known subject. Check your local PBS schedule for broadcast times. To order a DVD, please contact Smith Farms at 270-841-0736 or Billy Smith at 270-489-6166, or e-mail whsmith@wk.net

BIBLIOGRAPHY

Bennett, Tevis. "Billy Smith is New AFBF Young People's Chairman." Farm Bureau News. January 1965.

Berry, Wendell. Tobacco Harvest: An Elegy. University Press of Kentucky. 2004.

Breen, T. H. Tobacco Culture: The Mentality of the Great aTidewater Planters on the Eve of Revolution. Princeton University Press. 1985.

Clark, Thomas D. Agrarian Kentucky. The University Press of Kentucky. 1977.

Clark, Thomas D. A History of Kentucky. The Jesse Stuart Foundation. 1988 ed.

Clark, Thomas D. Kentucky: Land of Contrast. New York: Harper and Row 1968.

Cooper, Dorothea C. Kentucky Hospitality: A 200-Year Tradition. Kentucky Federation of Women's Clubs, Inc. 1976.

Cunningham, Bill. On Bended Knees: The Night Rider Story. McClanahan Publishing House, Incorporated. 1983.

Fox, Virginia. Clark's Kentucky Almanac and Book of Facts 2006. The Clark Group. 2005.

Gassett, Jon. Clark's Kentucky Almanac and Book of Facts 2006. The Clark Group. 2005

Jennings, Dorothy and Kirby. The Story of Calloway County 1822-1976. Murray Democrat Publishing Co. 1980 ed.

Kleber, John E. Thomas D. Clark, Lowell H. Harrison, and James C. Klotter. Kentucky Encyclopedia. The University Press of Kentucky. 1992.

Klotter, James C. Kentucky Portrait in Paradox, 1900-1950. The Kentucky Historical Society. 1996.

Rouse, Jr., Parke. The Great Wagon Road: From Philadelphia to the South. The Dietz Press. 2004 ed.

"One Room Schools." <u>Recollections of Calloway County.</u> Honor's IV English 1990. page 107.

Smith, Hal. "School News." <u>Kirksey High School Echo.</u> Kirksey High School. October 1930.

Smith, Hal. "Don't Give Up the Ship." <u>Kirksey High School Echo.</u> Kirksey High School. October 1930.

Nightrider Articles. <u>Murray Ledger and Times.</u> February 22, 1908. March 8, 1908, April 2, 1908.

Roadbed Articles Murray Ledger and Times. 1913.

"Kirksey FFA." <u>Murray Ledger and Times.</u> 1954.

"Basketball." <u>Kirksey High School Echo.</u> Kirksey High School. November 1929.

"The Farmers Problem." <u>Kirksey High School Echo.</u> Kirksey High School. June 30, 1929.

"Farmers' Short Course at Kirksey." <u>Kirksey High School Echo.</u> Kirksey High School. January 1930.

"Sitting on Top of the World." <u>Kirksey High School Echo.</u> Kirksey High School. January 1930.

"Some Things to Think About – Calloway Needs County Agent." <u>Kirksey High School Echo.</u> Kirksey High School. January 1930.

The School Paper." <u>Kirksey High School Echo.</u> Kirksey High School. October 25, 1929.

"You're Welcome." <u>Kirksey High School Echo.</u> Kirksey High School. June 30, 1929 .

1949 Chevrolet pick up 154, 155

1951 Plymouth 154, 155, 188

1955 red belly Ford tractor 158

20-gauge Browning 145

606 Sycamore Street 159, 160

8000 Ford tractor 173

A

Agrarian Kentucky 24, 48, 93, 194

Agri-Chem 188

Agri-Power 188

Agricultural Adjustment Act (AAA) 62

Agriculture Committee 190

agriculture loan officer 165

Agri Port Terminal 188

American Farm Bureau 157, 167, 168, 185

American Farm Bureau Federation 157, 185

American Farm Bureau Young People's Committee 168, 185

American Farmer Degree 168

American Tobacco Company 45

Antarctica IV, 189

Armed Forces 7

Asbury graveyard 125, 129

Association 46, 47, 50, 51

B

'Billy Yank' 126

'bluebook' 126

Backusburg Hill 69

bales 67, 77, 128, 177

Ballard County Refuge 147

Banana Festival 85

Bank of Murray 166

Barbie doll 131

Barkley Lake 147

basketball 96, 143, 150, 151, 159

Baton Rouge, Louisiana 91

Battle, J. H. 43

Battle of the Bulge 52

Bazzell, Bobby 183

Bazzell, Charlie 102

Bazzell, Howard and Sue 102, 103

Belgium 146

bell peppers 175

Benton 172

Berry, Wendell 194

Bird hunting 147

Black Patch War 45, 50, 55

Blakley, R.W. 163, 165, 166

Blue Boar Cafeteria 100, 101

Blue Ridge Mountains 1

Boone, Daniel 12

Bowling Green, Ky. 184

Breeding, Michael 191

Brewer, Carl 18, 19, 36

Brewer, Clay 19, 36, 100

Brewer, Clyde 19, 36

Brewer, Dovie Sutherland 18, 19, 106

Brewer, Floy 122

Brewer, Irvin 19, 36

Brewer, James Irvin 18, 19

Brewer, Jim 36

Brewer, Jodie 19

Brewer, Joe 36

Brewer, Linnie 100, 104

Brewer, Lois Robinson 15, 18, 20, 21, 39, 57, 58, 67, 68, 94, 119, 122, 129, 132, 136

Brewer, Sam 15, 19, 36, 37, 39, 57, 59, 66, 67, 68, 69, 100, 121, 122, 127, 129, 132, 135, 136, 137, 141, 157, 158, 163

Brewer's Cemetery 54

Brewers 150

Brewer side 51

bridal fashions 179

Broach, Ray 102

Brooks, Hamp 169

Brown, Sharon Story 129, 130, 179

Bryant, Bobbie Smith I, 8, 9, 18, 26, 30, 34, 59, 101, 102, 103, 104, 106, 109, 111, 119, 127, 131, 132, 134, 135, 136, 137, 139, 140, 141, 144, 151, 161, 181, 182

Bryant, Jr., William Hamilton (Bill) 9, 28, 63, 85

Buenos Aires 189

burlesque 126, 127

Butkus, Dick 146

C

Cain place 88, 111, 137, 162, 164

Calloway Countians 44, 45, 47

Calloway County III, 3, 5, 10, 12, 14, 15, 22, 24, 35, 37, 38, 44, 45, 46, 47, 51, 54, 55, 57, 59, 62, 63, 65, 79, 80, 81, 84, 90, 93, 94, 95, 96, 99, 102, 103, 104, 105, 107, 112, 114, 120, 123, 126, 127, 151, 153, 157, 158, 167, 168, 176, 183, 187, 194, 195

Calloway County Farm Bureau 167

Calloway County King 158

Calloway County Middle School 10, 105

Calloway County Normal College 94, 96, 103, 104

Calloway County Schools 10, 102

Calloway Needs County Agent 62, 195

Canada 86

Case self-propelled combine 171

Cessna 90

Cherokee 11

Chicago, Ill. 85, 167, 175, 190

Chicago Board of Trade 190

chicken house 137, 162

Chilcutt, Charles 147

Chilcutt, Evelyn Ahart Wilson 134

Chilcutt, Porter 111, 112, 131, 134, 140, 147

Chilcutt, Rubye Maynard 20, 111

Christian County 49, 60, 86, 175

Christmas 31, 97, 105, 129, 130, 131, 132, 134, 160

Civilian Conservation Crops 62

Civil War 22, 43, 44, 45, 48, 49, 93

Clark, Dr. Charles 169

Clark, Dr. Thomas 24, 30, 48, 93, 121

Clark, James 5

Clark's Kentucky Almanac 143, 194

Clark's River 12

Cleaver, Junior 179

Cocker Spaniel Jim 139

Coldwater 117

Coleman, Charles 158, 159

Coleman, Zane 163

Colonel Sanders 35

Commonwealth 3, 5

Confederacy 49

Confederate States 45

Congress 59, 81

Conservation Reserve Program 171

Constitution of the Kentucky High School Athletic Association 150

Con Wood 83

Cooper's Warehouse 86

Cooperative Extension Service 22

Corinth 95

Cox, Noble and Jonnie 167

Craig, Robert 183

Crossville, Tennessee 91

Cumberland Gap 3, 11, 12

Cumberland River 144

Cunningham, Bill 194

Cunningham, John 31, 34, 160, 164, 165

D

Dairy Dip 169

Dairy Queen 151, 156

dark fired tobacco 1, 16, 45, 84, 184

Dark Fired Tobacco Association 59

deer 15, 121, 143, 145, 146

Democratic Party 50

Depression 55, 57, 65, 79, 153

Detroit, Mich. 51, 65

Dixie Flyer 86

Doran, Harold 165, 166, 167, 180

DOT 178

Draughn's Business College 57, 58, 97

Duke, James B. 45

Dunn, Joe 35, 145, 171, 172

DuPont paint 65

E

Easley, Sid IV

Easter 132, 141, 160

Eddyville, Ky. 154, 155

Edmonds, G.W. 160, 164, 165

Eldridge, Leroy 126

Ellers, Fran I

Ellis, Harvey 100, 101, 126, 158, 165, 166, 167, 184

Ellis, Herman K. 183

Encyclopedia Britannica 124

EPA 178

F

Falwell, Timmy 174

Farm Bureau 9, 90, 91, 131, 157, 158, 167, 168, 185, 194

Farm Land Bank program 171

Farm Security Administration 62

Federal army 45

ferry 13

fertilizer industry 9

First Christian 24

fishing 143, 144

Five and Dime Store 57

Fletcher, Gov. Ernie 188

football 10, 99, 137, 143, 146, 151, 152, 175

Ford Motor Company 51, 65, 66

France 11, 54

Frankfort, Ky. I, 44, 49, 190

Fulton, Ky. 85

Future Farmers of America (FFA) 100, 126, 158, 168, 184, 195

G

Gadsden, Alabama 91

Gardner, Elmo 108

Gator 10, 89

General Assembly 5

General Tire 169

German 1, 11, 12, 40

Germany 11, 52

Ginger 141

Gingles, C. O. 66

Gingles, Johnny 16, 50

Girl Scouts 10

Go Slow Mary 96

grandmother Dot 143

Grand Old Opry 34, 52

grapes 189

Graves County 3, 30, 190

Great Depression 55, 57, 79, 153

Great Wagon Road 1, 2, 11, 12, 194

Greenfield, Tenn. 109

Greenville, Miss. 91

Greyhound Bus 87

Growers Association 49

Grubbs, Ida 40

Grubbs, Lovie 40

Grubbs, William 40

H

H2A program 178, 190

Halloween 127, 128, 129

Halls, Tennessee 7, 52

Happy New Year 97

Harding School 93

Harvey, Paul 168

hay 67, 98, 163, 177

He's My Pal 96

helicopter 91, 92, 109, 110

Henry, Lt. Governor Steve 187

Hereford cows 161

Herndon, Woody 91, 92, 110

Hickman 148

hog III, 56, 106, 118, 119, 121, 134

Holt, Crawford Duncan 80, 81

Homemaker's Clubs 20

Hopkinsville, Ky. 46, 181, 182, 184, 188

Hunt, Wayne 188

Hunting 143

Hurt, Brandon 46

Hurt, Max 102

Hurt, Max and Mavis 27, 28

Hutson, Dan 91, 169, 170

Hutson Chemical Company 22, 86, 87, 90, 91, 92, 107, 109, 110, 112, 166, 169, 170, 173, 180

I

I Choose to be Happy: A School Shooting Survivor's Triumph Over Tragedy 191

Illinois 44, 177

Imes, Kenny 39

Indians 22, 37, 140

J

J. H. Churchill's Funeral Home 39

Jackson Purchase III, 11, 44, 183

James, George 109, 110

James, Joe Pat 25

Jaycee's Distinguished Service Award for Calloway County 168

Jennings, Dorothy and Kirby 14, 24

Johnson, Shorty 26

Jones, Diane 26

Jones, Greg 26

Jones, John 26

Jones, Nadine 26

K

K.H.S. Eagles 97, 150

Kail, Johnathan (John) Robert 7

Kail, Joshua (Josh) Arnold 7

Kail, Kelley Blair Phillips 7

Kaintuckee 11

Kansas City, Missouri 28, 126, 168

Kenlake International 170

Kentuckians 121

Kentucky I, III, V, 1, 3, 4, 5, 9, 10, 11, 12, 13, 14, 16, 17, 22, 23, 24, 30, 34, 35, 40, 43, 44, 45, 47, 48, 49, 55, 56, 57, 62, 64, 65, 77, 80, 83, 86, 87, 93, 101, 106, 109, 118, 119, 121, 122, 125, 129, 143, 144, 145, 147, 149, 150, 152, 158, 168, 170, 173, 182, 183, 184, 185, 187, 188, 190, 194

Kentucky: Land of Contrast 30, 86, 121, 125, 194

Kentucky: Portrait in Paradox 57, 62

Kentucky Constitution 93

Kentucky Encyclopedia 13, 22, 40, 106, 194

Kentucky Farm Bureau 185

Kentucky governor 188

Kentucky Historical Society (KHS) I, 12, 17, 55, 56, 60, 77, 95, 96, 101, 104, 107, 118, 150, 158, 194

Kentucky Hospitality: A 200 Year Tradition 22, 122

Kentucky Lake 147, 170, 173

Kentucky League of Cities 9

Kentucky State Fair 101, 152, 158, 184

Kentucky State Guard 43

Kentucky State Militia 43

Kentucky Woodland National Wildlife Refuge 143

Kirk, Dorothy 143

Kirksey 7, 15, 16, 24, 25, 26, 27, 28, 29, 30, 31, 32, 33, 34, 39, 46, 50, 54, 55, 57, 60, 61, 62, 63, 64, 65, 66, 68, 94, 95, 96, 97, 98, 101, 102, 103, 104, 107, 109, 111, 114, 126, 127, 128, 137, 146, 150, 152, 153, 154, 157, 158, 159, 161, 167, 169, 180, 184, 185, 188, 195

Kirksey, Stephen 15

Kirksey Ball Park 152

Kirksey Bank 16

Kirksey community 7, 15, 27, 46, 55, 63, 68, 94, 95, 127, 161

Kirksey Critter 153, 185

Kirksey Future Farmers of America (FFA) Chapter 98, 107, 184

Kirksey High School 27, 60, 61, 62, 94, 95, 96, 97, 98, 101, 104, 126, 127, 150, 159, 195

Kirksey High School Echo 60, 62, 95, 195

Kirksey Highway 68, 111, 161, 180

Kirksey School 95, 102, 103

Kirksey store 50, 146, 188

Kirksey tornado 111

Kirksey United Methodist Church 25, 26, 27, 28, 54, 96

Klondyke 107, 108

Kniffin, G. C. 44

Kopperud, Dr. A. H. 183

Kyle, Verne 90

L

Labor Day 165

Lawrence, Ocus 30

Lee School 98

Lenin, Toy 90, 91

Lieutenant governor 188

Little Rock, Ark. 154

Little Rock Church 25

Little Rock School 24, 25, 93, 94, 95

Louisville & Nashville Railroad 86

Louisville, Ky. 1, 86, 90, 91, 100, 101, 125, 126, 184

Louis XIV of France 11

Lovett, Wells 103

Lynn Grove 97

Lynn Grove Egg Company 162

M

Marshall basketeers 150

Marshall County 2, 3, 5, 12, 13, 43, 54, 56

Marshall County Genealogical and Historical Society 43

Marshall County Kentucky 43

Martin Oil 173

Maryland 1

Mathis' Orchard 35

Mayfield 7, 25, 30, 31, 35, 44, 52, 54, 57, 58, 63, 68, 98, 99, 100, 129, 130, 137, 139, 169, 172

Mayfield Middle School 100

McCallon, Janetta 109

McCallon, Jewell 107

McCallon, Margaret 34

McCallon, Martha 34

McCallon, Monice 106

McCallon, Nitarie 109

McCallon, Randy 109

McConnell, Sen. Mitch 83

McCracken County school system 104

McDougall, R. Pierce 183

Memphis, Tenn. 34, 169, 184

Metcalfe, Thomas 3

Methodist 8, 24, 25, 26, 27, 39, 54, 96, 97

Mexican workers 114, 115, 178

Mexico 17, 84

Middle Fork Creek 3

Mid South Fair 184

milk man 164

Minneapolis, Minn. 66, 85

Minneapolis Moline tractor 66

Mississippi River 17

Missouri 44, 110, 126

Model T 68

Montell, Brad 105

Moonlight Schools 93

Morgan, Dave 48

Mormon 24

Mr. Palmer 174

Mr. Washer 129

Murray 15, 21, 33, 39, 44, 45, 46, 47, 48, 49, 56, 57, 59, 64, 65, 78, 87, 90, 91, 95, 101, 102, 103, 104, 112, 126, 152, 156, 159, 160, 163, 166, 167, 169, 172, 179, 180, 186, 189, 191, 194, 195

Murray airport 91

Murray City School system 102

Murray High School 104

Murray Hospital 112

Murray Ledger and Times 46, 47, 48, 56, 65, 101, 195

Murray Manufacturing 90

Murray State Normal School 45, 104

Murray State Teachers College 95

Murray State University 102, 103, 104, 152, 191

Murray Stock Yards 163

Murray Training School 126

N

Nana's Best Goose Dressing 149

Nanny, Lester 169

Nanny goat 136

Nashville, Tenn. 34, 86

Nation's Agriculture 157, 167, 185

National FFA 126

New Deal 62

New Orleans 17, 85, 86, 110

New Year 57, 97, 134, 135

Night Riders 45, 46, 47, 48, 49, 50, 51

Nip 142, 143

North Carolina 2, 3, 11, 12, 16

O

Oak Level 3

Ohio River 91

Oliver, Milton 49

Omaha, Nebraska 27

OSHA regulations 178

outhouse 58, 59, 94, 127, 128

Outland, Charles 183

Overby, George Ed 161

Overland Park, Kansas 152

Owensboro, Ky. 83

P

Pace, Hershel 26

Paducah, Ky. 28, 52, 57, 97, 105, 137, 191

Paducah High School, 1997 137, 191

Palmer, Baron 26

Palmer place 174

Parrish, Elvin Lee 171

Parrish, Lubie 26, 102, 171, 172, 173

Parrish, Reba Faye 102, 171, 172, 173

Parrish, Rob Edd 171, 174

Parrish family 172, 173

Paschall, Martha 180

Pathfinder 94

Patsy 140

Penny 64, 90, 121, 163

Penny Highway 163

People's Bank 165, 166, 180

Perrin, H. H. 43

Phillip Morris Tobacco Company 83

Phillips, Robert (Bob) 7

Phillips, Susan Smith 7, 32, 52

Piedmont region of North Carolina 2, 12

pimento peppers 176

Piper Navaho 91

Plant beds 163

Planters Protective Association 45, 79

Plymouth 68

Presbyterian 24

President Truman 168

Primitive Baptist Church 7

Prudential Life Insurance Company 163

Q

quail 15, 143

Quilting Bees 20

quota system 81

R

R. J. Reynolds Tobacco Company 83

rabbits 141, 142

Recollections of Calloway County 99, 127, 195

Reed, Z.P. 25

Reeder, Jo 180

reforestation 62

Reid 15

Reidville 15

Republican Party 50

rescue squad 172

Robinson, Bertha Neal Wilson 38

Robinson, Bruce 38

Robinson, James Polk 39

Robinson, Lois 38

Robinson, Talmadge 38

Rogers, Van and Gloria 152

Roosevelt, Pres. Franklin D. 59, 79

Rosedale 15

Rouse, Jr., Parke 2, 12

Rudolph, Lt. Gov. Robbie 188

Ruiz, Bernadino 17

Rural Electric Corporation 64

rural mail carrier 163

Ryan Milk Plant 171

S

Santa Claus 130, 132

Santiago, Chile 189

Senators 81

Shawnee 11

Shelbyville, Ky. 109, 181

Shenandoah Valley of Virginia 1, 11

Shot, Jan 90, 91

Silent Brigade 45

Simmons, Audrey 163, 165

Smith, Absalom 2, 3, 5, 6, 43

Smith, Adam 2

Smith, Barbara 2

Smith, Bert 95, 104

Smith, Bessie 40

Smith, Bettie 8, 21, 28, 33, 39, 67, 96, 104, 105, 127, 130, 132, 151

Smith, Billy III, 3, 8, 15, 26, 30, 34, 37, 44, 50, 51, 52, 57, 58, 63, 65, 66, 68, 69, 71, 75, 78, 79, 83, 85, 86, 87, 89, 90, 92, 96, 98, 99, 100, 104, 107, 109, 110, 111, 118, 122, 123, 126, 127, 128, 129, 130, 134, 135, 136, 137, 139, 140, 145, 147, 148, 150, 152, 154, 155, 157, 158, 159, 160, 161, 162, 164, 167, 168, 169, 171, 179, 183, 184, 185, 188, 189, 194

Smith, Billy Dale 8, 9, 10, 18, 21, 29, 30, 33, 34, 36, 37, 64, 67, 69, 70, 71, 72, 73, 74, 75, 76, 77, 87, 88, 89, 101, 102, 103, 104, 105, 106, 107, 108, 111, 113, 116, 117, 121, 128, 131, 132, 134, 136, 137, 139, 140, 141, 142, 145, 147, 148, 149, 153, 154, 155, 156, 161, 162, 171, 173, 175, 177, 178, 185, 186, 187, 188, 189, 190

Smith, Burton 3, 6, 14, 43, 55

Smith, Carter 10, 26, 37

Smith, Delle 6, 7, 40, 119

Smith, Eli 2

Smith, Eliza 3

Smith, Elizabeth 3, 11

Smith, Emma Grubbs 6, 7, 40

Smith, Evelyn Vaden 7, 32, 52, 54

Smith, Geneva Brewer 7, 18, 21, 24, 27, 28, 29, 34, 36, 38, 57, 64, 68, 69, 75, 76, 93, 105, 108, 109, 119, 122, 133, 134

Smith, Gracie Wrather 7, 16, 25, 30, 31, 32, 33, 40, 50, 52, 54, 65, 119, 130

Smith, Hal 6, 7, 8, 27, 29, 30, 32, 33, 34, 40, 52, 58, 65, 66, 76, 87, 88, 89, 96, 97, 98, 102, 103, 104, 105, 134, 138, 150, 151, 157, 195

Smith, Haleene 6, 7, 40, 104, 119

Smith, Henry 1, 2, 3, 11, 12, 14, 16, 43, 104

Smith, James 7, 8, 32, 40, 52, 53, 54, 65

Smith, James Franklin 6, 7, 104

Smith, Janae 9, 10, 71, 89, 152

Smith, John 3, 43

Smith, Josh 9, 10, 20, 26, 33, 37, 42, 71, 73, 75, 76, 88, 105, 114, 115, 117, 124, 134, 135, 138, 142, 143, 145, 146, 151, 154, 155, 156, 171, 174, 176, 191

Smith, Levina 3

Smith, Lillian 6, 7

Smith, Logan 9, 10, 26, 37

Smith, Martha Adeline 6

Smith, Mary Ann 3

Smith, Mary Elizabeth 6

Smith, Melissa (Missy) Jenkins 10, 26, 105, 191

Smith, Nancy Caroline 6

Smith, Needham Van Buren 3, 6, 43, 55

Smith, Nellie 2

Smith, Paul 40

Smith, Raymon 3, 6, 7, 25, 30, 31, 32, 33, 40, 52, 54, 65, 66, 67, 75, 76, 104, 130, 158, 163, 165

Smith, Rebecca L. 6

Smith, Rex 6, 40

Smith, Robert 40

Smith, Sally 2

Smith, Sara 3

Smith, Sheila Kirk 10, 18, 134

Smith, Shirley 8, 9, 18, 20, 31, 32, 36, 38, 85, 90, 91, 101, 102, 103, 108, 110, 111, 112, 119, 127, 134, 135, 136, 137, 140, 149, 154, 155, 156, 157, 159, 160, 161, 163, 164, 165, 166, 168, 169, 171, 172, 179, 180, 181, 182, 187

Smith, Sue 40

Smith, William 3

Smith, William Aaron 6

Smith, William Hal 7, 8

Smith family I, III, 1, 3, 10, 11, 12, 14, 15, 17, 20, 21, 23, 24, 25, 30, 39, 40, 52, 54, 68, 74, 78, 79, 84, 93, 94, 104, 105, 123, 127, 128, 132,

134, 135, 136, 139, 143, 144, 157, 167, 172, 173, 183, 185, 190

Smith Farms 1, 9, 10, 14, 17, 54, 72, 73, 74, 80, 105, 113, 115, 125, 129, 134, 174, 175, 178, 188, 191

Smith men 31, 55, 153

Smith women 179

smokeless tobacco 84

snipe hunting 123, 124

Snowball 139

Snow geese 149

Soil Conservation Administration 62

Soldier Creek 2, 3, 7, 12

Southern Bell Company 64

South Pacific 52

Southwest Airlines 87

soybeans 1, 21, 34, 172, 189

Spanish 177

Springville, Tennessee 173

St. Louis, Missouri 34, 179

Staley (Stahli), Elizabeth 1, 2

state and federal farm regulations 178

State Highway Department 128

state representative 190

Stella 161

Stoll, Bettie Smith 8, 28, 33, 39, 67, 96, 105, 119, 127, 151

Stoll, Gregg 8

Stoll, Sarah 8

Stoll, Suzannah 8

Story, Harvey 58, 129, 130, 150

Story, Jo Nell 58, 129, 130

Story, Reva Brewer 24, 39, 57, 58, 68, 93, 109, 129

suckers 72

Suiter, Larry 183

Suiter, Shelby Parker 158

Superman 92

Sutherland, Dale 153

Szabo, Suzannah Stoll 8, 152

Szabo, Tim 8

Szabo, Zachary 8

T

Tapia, Luis 72

Taylor, Diana 1

Taylor Gray Communications 1

telephone cooperative 64

Tennessee 5, 7, 12, 13, 17, 44, 45, 52, 62, 73, 83, 109, 143, 144, 170, 175, 182

Tennessee River 17, 144

Tennessee Valley Authority (TVA) 62, 143

Texaco Service Station 131

Texas 177

Thanksgiving III, 118, 132, 137

The Echo 96

The New Deal Administration 62

The Showcase 117, 165, 166, 167, 171, 173, 179, 180, 181

The Story of Calloway County 14, 24, 35, 37, 38, 47, 51, 59, 79, 80, 93, 194

Time To Behold: Triumph Over Tragedy by Faith, Prayers and a Positive Attitude 187

tobacco III, 1, 9, 10, 12, 16, 17, 34, 42, 45, 46, 47, 48, 51, 57, 59, 60, 61, 62, 63, 65, 67, 69, 70, 71, 72, 73, 74, 75, 76, 77, 78, 79, 80, 81, 82, 83, 84, 86, 87, 97, 98, 106, 107, 112, 113, 114, 115, 129, 138, 154, 157, 158, 159, 160, 161, 163, 169, 174, 175, 176, 177, 178, 183, 184

tobacco buyout 82, 83, 86

tobacco floor 77, 161, 169

tobacco hogsheads 86

tobacco market 57, 176

Tobacco Planters Protective Association 45

tobacco production 70, 175

tobacco scaffolds 129

Today's Smith Farms 1, 14

tractor pulls 143, 153

Tri-City 151

Tucker, Randy 153

Turner, William T. 49, 60, 86

U

U. S. Department of Agriculture 61

U.S. government 79, 83, 178

U.S. Tobacco Company 83

Union 43, 50

Used Car Capital 153

Utterback School 99

V

VAC Case tractor 158

Vaughn, Jane 159

Venable 151

Virginia 1, 12, 43, 194

volleyball 10, 152

W

Wadesboro (Waidsboro) 3, 24, 56

Washer, Jim 161

waterfowl 143, 147

Wells, County Judge A.J.G. 47

Wells, Rainey T. 95, 103

Western Tobacco Warehouse Association 86

West Kentucky I, V, 1, 10, 12, 13, 23, 43, 44, 45, 64, 65, 83, 87, 119, 143, 182, 183, 187, 188, 190

West Kentucky Rural Telephone Cooperative 64

west Tennessee 83, 182

wheat 1, 21, 34, 55, 98, 128, 172

wild turkey 143

Wilson, Albert 183

Wilson, Bill David 156

Wilson, Governor A.E. 47, 48

Wilson, Stub 91

Wilsonian Society 97

Wisehart, Bernice 22

Woodmen of the World 27

World War I 50, 51, 55

World War II 9, 51, 55, 129

worming tobacco 72

Wrather, Ada 119

Wrather, Gratis 50, 51, 65

Wrather, William 16

CPSIA information can be obtained at www.ICGtesting.com
Printed in the USA
LVOW131320291012

304906LV00006B/19/P